WOMEN—MARCH TOWARDS DIGNITY

Social and Legal Perspectives

Edited by :
KUSUM

Foreword :
JUSTICE RAJINDAR SACHAR
Former, Chief Justice, Delhi High Court
Chairman PUCL; Member, U.N. Sub-committee on Human Rights

Regency Publications
New Delhi

ISBN 81-86030-04-2

Published by Regency Publications, 20/36-G, Old Market, West Patel Nagar, New Delhi-110008 and printed at Radiant Printers, New Delhi-110008, Phone : 5713968, 5783571.

FOREWORD

It gives me a great pleasure to write the Foreword for this book "Women : March Towards Dignity—Social and Legal Perspectives" edited by a well known erudite scholar Ms. Kusum of the Indian Law Institute. She has chosen the various topics with great care with a view to present the problems of women in the country from different perspectives.

Justice Iyer in his article, "Human Right to be Woman" laments the denial of gender justice inspite of high flying oratory in public life. It is, however, some matter of gratification that the National Commission for Women was set up in 1992. Mr. P.M. Bakshi's article dealing with "Family Courts" brings out the various facets which the Family Courts Act is supposed to subserve from the procedural angle. Despite the Family Courts Act 1984, no proper infrastructure has been provided by the Government to the Judiciary so that it would become a real effective forum as it was meant to be. Thus it is a matter of regret that Family Courts have not been established in Delhi. Wherever they have been established, it is merely a change of nomenclature from the existing District Courts dealing with matrimonial matters to what are now called the Family Courts. Greater involvement of social scientists and jurists is necessary to make this piece of legislation an effective instrument.

Mr. Krishan Mahajan is critical about the compartmentalised approach to women under the Indian Constitution which promises justice (social, economic and political), liberty, equality and fraternity for all Indian citizens regardless of whether they are men or women.

Besides, the editor has also included important areas of socio-legal aspects. Particular mention needs to be made to the Late Justice V.S. Deshpande's contribution, "Monogamy in India" wherein he has focussed on fraud on the law due to frivolous conversions and easily obtainable divorce decrees from foreign jurisdictions. Another article deals with the purely legalistic approach in matters of conflict of laws in matrimonial jurisdiction based on husband's domicile.

The article on "Irretrievable Breakdown of Marriage" points out the probable pros and cons of the ground for divorce in India. The editor has appended a note in favour of incorporating breakdown as a ground for divorce. The editor has also brought in the idea of remunerative home management by another author. Included also are articles on socio-legal aspects in the context of minor brides, female offenders, abortion and restitution of conjugal rights.

The book has been brought out in a very presentable manner. The choice of subjects range with very great thought. I have no doubt that the reader would be greatly benefited by the information, knowledge and the style of the various articles.

New Delhi (Rajindar Sachar)

PREFACE

It was my desire to bring out a book in the memory of my mother, who was a prolific writer in her own right. Issues relating to women and children were her special concern. Thus was conceived the idea and theme of the present book, which however, is just an humble drop in the vast ocean of literature on women.

The book is a collection of articles on various issues related to women. I am extremely grateful to Hon'ble Justice Krishna Iyer, Prof. P.M. Bakshi, Prof. Sivaramayya, Mr. Krishan Mahajan and my other friends who readily responded to my request for contributions. I wish to make a special mention of Late Justice V.S. Deshpande, who was the first person with whom I shared my idea of the book. He not only encouraged me but, inspite of health problems, was the first person to give an article.

I owe special thanks to Ms. Lakshmi Jambholkar who, apart from her valuable article, has given great help in bringing out this book.

September 1993

Kusum

CONTENTS

HUMAN RIGHT TO BE WOMAN

*Justice Krishna Iyer**

"Mine are the tears
that froze with the pain
mine is the pain
that has no name"

The Indian Constitution advocates social justice, a poignant component of which is gender justice. What is demanded is not charity nor grace nor as legal aid to a weaker sex. The militant claim is the woman's right to be oneself, not a doll to please, nor an inmate of a workhouse. She has the human right to be woman. The personality of one's sister cannot be warped to suit the masculine ethos nor shaped to confer pseudo-freedom, keeping subordination as an unwritten code of the suppressed tribe.

From the latest Tirupati Congress elections to the non-starter project of the Women's Statutory Commission, all that is done in favour of women is to bluff through double-speak baloney and conceal the indignity of her shame.

Let me quote a few verses from "VIMOCHANA" which has always fought the cause of the victim sister and the vintage culture of sex injustice. The right to life belongs to women too.

"Remember me ?
I was also your neighbour
whose silent screams you heard
through carefully closed windows
and whose bruise marks you saw
through deliberately unseeing eyes."

*Former Judge, Supreme Court of India

"If I rebelled against the injustice
I became a 'bajaari'
When perchance I laughed out in joy
if only to seek slivers of strength
I became a 'loose woman'."

"Can you help rewrite my story?
Can you throw open your windows
and quite simply—reach out?
"I want to sing another song
not a dirge
but a melody that soars with my desire
to live."

In that song, all humanists must join the chorus, because man and woman are human, are together one, equal but independent in personality. A new demand for empowerment of women preceded by a performance audit of the failures and frauds is the first step.

Gender Justice—An Unpleasant Performance Audit

"The history of mankind is a history of repeated injuries and usurpations on the part of man toward woman, having in direct object the establishment of a tyranny over her."[1]

The politics of women's emancipation since Indian Independence, has not made that quantum jump which the militant struggle, under Gandhi and Nehru, and the Government by a powerful lady, Indira Gandhi, would have led one to expect. Speaking from a global point of view, the status of women has made tardy headway even in the Soviet Union, as revealed in reports after the glasnost age, the situation being much worse in the West and the Orient. The U.S. has failed to ratify into its constitution equality of the sexes. This is not to deny the factum of the march of womanhood. In all spheres of life there is a general realisation in our century that the measure of a nation's progress is the advance registered by its women. "There will never be a generation of great men until there has been a generation of free women"—wrote Robert Ingersoll, but quotations from noble soul and rhetoric in Commission Reports do not take wings unless the hardware of effective action resulting in actual transformation is produced. Women in India have, notwithstanding legend and scripture, suffered for long centuries. No single religion has spared her. The social and legal culture vis a vis the female gender has not elevated her to an equal level, breaking with the past, insisting on egalite and making her role autonomous. Women's 'vimochana', in its semantic fullness and as a personality development project, is still distances away from her. Whatever the paramount parchment of the Constitution may intone, whatever the universal instruments may inscribe, we have miles to go and promises to keep if Gender Justice is not to be mere dope but sure hope.

The battle for Swaraj found women participate in good measure against the British, against social suppression, against legal inhibition and economic deprivation. Indian Independence was value-loaded beyond political liberation and the Constitution condensed the imperatives of Gender Justice into Fundamental Rights and Directive Principles of State Policy. The supreme lex, in its various articles, not only mandates equality of the sexes but also authorizes benign discrimination in favour of women and children to make up for the backwardness which has been their age-old *kismet*. But categorical imperatives, constitutionalised by the Founding Fathers, are not self-acting but must acquire socio-legal locomotion by appropriate State action. With the objective of making a comprehensive survey of the yawning gap between what is and what ought to be - poignant reality and promise of equality—a high-powered Committee was appointed to go into the status of women in India and to make recommendations for elimination of those disabilities and injustices which handicapped their long march to their destined destination, individually and collectively. The Report of the Committee has been preserved with great care by Government since the end of 1974 and the time comes 15 years later to assess and audit the progress of the shortfall. Phulrenu Guha, the Chairperson, happy that her Report coincided with the celebration of the International Women's Year, drew attention to one unhappy circumstance: "our investigation has revealed that large masses of women in this country have remained unaffected by the rights guaranteed to them by the Constitution and the laws enacted since Independence". The recommendations are not radical but are informed by modest realism and moderate claims of Gender Justice, viewed in the light of evolving standards of women's status through universal instruments and United Nation's resolutions. Woman Unbound is a long distance from Womanhood home-bound or bonded surround.

No long is the Woman Question an insulated Indian issue, its wider dimensions demand an international essay and an evaluation of the Indian situation in the light of the emerging Women's Order.

A Gender Journey Within and Without our Country

Women, despite the printed rhetoric, suffer discrimination and indignity so damnable that dehumanisation is the gender reality of India. The World Human Order finds women's status high on the agenda of change.

> "The United Nations is committed to the principle of equality of men and women, meaning equality in their dignity and worth as human beings as well as equality in their rights, opportunities and responsibilities. In its work for the advancement of women, the entire United Nations system has dedicated itself to ensuring the universal recognition, in law, of equality of rights between men and women, and to exploring ways to give women, in fact, equal opportunities with men to realize their human rights and fundamental freedoms."[2]

The U.N. instruments, with focus on women's emancipation, include:

> "The Declaration on the Elimination of Discrimination against Women (1967), the Declaration of Mexico on the Equality of Women and Their Contribution to Development and Peace (1975) and the Convention on the Elimination of all Forms of Discrimination against Women (1979).
>
> "There are also a number of United Nations instruments which deal with problems that affect women adversely, including the Convention for the Suppression of the Traffic in Persons and of the Prostitution of Others (1949), the Convention on the Political Rights of Women (1952), the Supplemen-

tary Convention on the Abolition of Slavery, the Slave Trade, and Institutions and Practices similar to Slavery (1956).

"The General Conference of the International Labour Organisation has adopted instruments such as the Convention concerning the Employment of Women on Underground Work and in Mines of All Kinds, 1935 (No. 45), the Convention concerning Night Work of Women Employed in Industry (Revised, 1948) (No. 89), the Convention concerning Equal Remuneration for Men and Women Workers for work of Equal Value, 1951 (No. 100), the Convention concerning Discrimination in Respect of Employment and Occupation, 1958 (No. 111), and the Convention (No. 156) and Recommendation (No. 165) concerning equal Opportunities and Equal Treatment for Men and Women Workers: Worker with Family Responsibilities, 1981.

"The United Nations Education, Scientific and Cultural Organisation adopted the Convention against Discrimination in Education in 1960."[3]

Speaking of equality before the law, what is desiderated is not a mechanical or formal but dynamic jurisprudence of non-discrimination where gender is no disability and unfoldment of personality suffers no inhibition because of female sex. The U.N. Declaration on the Elimination of Discrimination against Women is a protest against masculine cultural arrogance, voiced in the Preamble that, "despite the Charter of the United Nations, the Universal Declaration of Human Rights, the International Covenants on Human Rights and other instruments of the United Nations and of the specialized agencies and despite the progress made in the matter of equality of rights, there continues to exist considerable discrimination against women." The Preamble points out that "discrimination against women is incompatible with human dignity and with the welfare of the family and of society, prevents their participation, on equal terms with men, in the political, social, economic and cultural life of their countries and is an obstacle to the full development of the potentialities of women in the service of their countries and of humanity". The fundamentally unjust insult to the dignity of women is condemned and equality affirmed in the Mexico Declaration of July 1975. From 1974 to 1979 more Conventions emphasise that discrimination is a comprehensive vice and covers "any distinction, exclusion or restriction made on the basis of sex which has the effect or purpose of impairing or nullifying the recognition, enjoyment or exercise by women, irrespective of their marital status, on a basis of equality of men and women, of human rights and fundamental freedoms in the political, economic, social, cultural, civil or any other field." On December 10, 1979 the U.N. adopted a comprehensive Convention on the Elimination of All Forms of Discrimination against Women. Part V thereof established a monitoring Committee.

Health, employment, participation in all fields, education and training modification of discriminatory municipal laws and so on are part of the equality package. Slavery is anathematised by the 'ECOSOCO' which defines, as similar to slavery "any institution or practice whereby : (i) a woman, without the right to refuse, is promised or given in marriage on payment of a consideration in money or in kind to her parents, guardian, family or any other person or group; or (ii) the husband of a woman, his family, or his clan, has the right to transfer her to another person for value received or otherwise; or (iii) a woman on the death of her husband is liable to be inherited by another person . . ."

High standards, high-falutin diction! But how vicious is the scenario of gender discrimination and human rights hypocrisy in the land of Sita sentenced to life in forest and Sati sentenced to incinerated death? Alas, woman everywhere faces the Sita-Sati syndrome. Let us look at the world scene for a while:

> "In 1980, on the recommendation of the Commission on the Status of women, the Economic and Social Council found that, in many countries, prosecuted, indicted or imprisoned women are often subjected to intolerable treatment and specific forms of torture, especially when they are harassed in violation of fundamental rights because of their national or racial origin, or solely on the basis of their political opinions.
>
> "Recalling Article 5 of the Universal Declaration of Human Rights and the Declaration on the Protection of All Persons from Being Subjected to Torture and Other Cruel, Inhuman or Degrading Treatment or Punishment, the council solemnly appealed to Governments and international bodies concerned with the defence of human rights to pay particular attention

to the conditions in which women are detained, especially concerning respect for their dignity and corporal integrity."[4]

Many international documents rich with egalitarian rhetoric notwithstanding, what is the reality of the quantum and quality of woman's human rights in Indiramma's India? I am unhappy I have to say hard things against the Indian Establishment despite its Constitution, because our sisters are rightless and must thank Heavens if they are left *alive* in Bharat Bhoomi! What a lurid contrast of pathos to read the international instruments of gender care and concern and the national denial, *de facto*, of even the right to life, to dignity and to those components of freedom which make a woman human!

Sati, the crime of murder by burning inflicted with fanatical heartlessness on wives who weep as their husbands lie dead, is practised by pushing, with religious fury, the victim wife into the funeral pyre as the flames consume the husband's corpse. The British banned it; Gandhi opposed it. Indian Judges read into it abetment of homicide but the majesty of the State winked at this popular festival of burning a woman as a funeral ritual. No case is registered, few prosecutions and government minions permit temples and worship in honour of the publicly murdered martyr. A redundant legislation was enacted when womankind shrieked in protest, but when Swami Agnivesh believed the State and its new law and journeyed to Rajasthan with its message he was arrested to prevent breakdown of 'law and order'! Hypocrisy! thy name is Indian Republic! Woman is equal under the law of course, but is non-person in praxis. A woman is a human without rights. To-day, held in thraldom by homicidal custom, womanhood dies in flames for her gender crime.

Sati is spiritualised murder but is first cousin to bridal murder dismissed dubiously as dowry death. How many brides are married to *yama* all over India, so tortured and doused in kerosene that death is deliverance from the marital habitat! Laws are made with blood-shot eyes to combat dowry, bride burning criminality and hara-kiri in despair, as social salve. But no damsels in distress are saved, few killers face trial, fewer are punished and fewest finally sentenced. Judges, invariably masculine custodians of criminal justice and its haunting rule of benefit of doubt, forget the burning *sister*, focus on the *male* dock, invoke the impossible rules against circumstantial evidence and remember that hundred guilty *men* may go free but the unknown innocent *man* shall not be punished. In dowry cases, all men are presumed innocent! Why? In a masculine legal system men have human rights but women have them writ in water. The police are men too! Their investigation bears gender bias, their custodial process betrays criminal manifestations. Even the prison keeps women insecure. For them the Constitution is counterfeit until gender justice turns militant, strident and honest.

Trafficking in women is slavery compounded with criminal commerce in humans. And yet that is common for the humbler women in primitive social penury. Do we dare to end the marketing of girls in weekly fairs in Madhya Pradesh and religious festivals a la Yellamma in Karnataka? Who constitute bonded labour? Adivasis, most of whom are women and children. Art. 23 commands that traffic in human beings and forms of forced labour are prohibited and punishable. And legislation exists to forbid these felonious practices. But they flourish. A stray purchase of a girl and produced in the Supreme Court made our jurisprudential boast blush. The Supreme Court breathed fire and brimstone but the adivasi belles' sales go on. The brokers know that judicial thunder need not be taken seriously. Such occasional noises are necessary to silence community conscience and for transnational consumption. Likewise, the bonded labour cases made the Supreme Court bark but not bite. It is part of the human rights game of hide and seek. Legislations against these horrendous evils are toothless because the legislators, the police, the courts and other agencies have patterned an unwitting conspiracy where the victims and villains remain where they are. Where women are involved, the legal dogs may bark but the criminal caravan will pass. When called upon to bark and also to bite the system fails as Operation Agnivesh demonstrates. The heroic swamiji suffered for taking the anti-sati law seriously. Gang rapes of adivasi girls by men, even policemen, are formally frowned upon by the new law; but if the law lies dead or the law is but lies, credibility dies. If episodes result in popular protest, belated but fruitless judicial enquiry may be the impotent end-product. Frailty and futility are open secrets where backward brackets, especially women, are concerned. They have no business to protest? And since the barbarity persists unabated, creative initiatives are needed to make the rule of law run close to the rule of life for that gender which, from foeticide, infanticide, dowrycide, saticide and suicide, has homicide of human rights writ large on her life. Far too long has the law hidden the truth of its printed lies and human justice written off as a lost cause.

If gender degradation is a social depravity and massive manslaughter of the human rights of womanhood a daily reality, then Indian culpability, as a community, is difficult to dispel. Substantive Law is dead if it loses its remedial potency. And it is no consolation to parade constitutional provisions and statute book pages if in raw life the woman is ever the victim. Let me put my observations emphatically, perhaps with some exaggeration, to drive home my point. After all, Oscar Wilde was right! "Moderation is a fatal thing; nothing succeeds like excess."

She is unjustly treated as unequal by society for the genetic sin of her discriminated sex. She suffers gender devaluation at home, at work, in literacy, in matrimony, in inheritance and allied rights, in economic opportunity, public life and power process. If she demands a right to her own personality she is punished and expelled, branded a mental case and lodged with lunatics, married off or sold, divorced or driven into the streets, victimised for dowry or forced into suicide or sati. Inside the lock-up or jail cell, or elsewhere in custody she is in sex peril, her peculiar needs ignored and family ties disowned. The system is the criminal, the woman bears the cross, the man the crown! The foeticidal, infanticidal, suicidal, lunatic and criminal syndromes accuse society of crime. What is the legal remedy for the gender malady?

We need the specifics of a technology to transform the cosmos of criminal justice and punitive praxis, charged with concern for the female handicaps and emphasis on woman's dignity and development. But this perspective of human *retrieval* is distances away. From harsh Macaulay to humane Mahatma is a long cultural haul vis a vis our prison process. To actualise this we need a police-prison culture with reverence for womanhood even if the person is criminally implicated or convicted. There must be built-in mechanisms which defend damsels in distress rather than harden them.

The adverse vicissitudes of women in custody are not stray phenomena but wide-spread and deep-rooted in the system. I have visited many penal and mental institutions in the South and some in the North and all of them share, in varying degrees, one major flaw, viz: that in the larger scheme, women do not matter or at least matter less, whatever the custodial institution.

Our sisters under domestic stress, sex discrimination or other causes wander in the streets or are wards in mental prisons. Have you seen the lunatic asylums in Calcutta, Calicut, Trichur or Ranchi? Institutions with lunacy in management writ large! Have you seen State-run Beggar Homes in any city, including affluent Bombay and quiet Cochin? Women who are neurotics, lepers, victims of miscellaneous diseases, domestic tragedies, poverty pathology and starvelings are lugged together with crass neglect and resourcelessness. And rehabilitative therapy and even basic decencies are absent! These institutions, not the inmates, are the criminals. They are a slur on our humanism, a slander on our culture, a rupture with our constitutional promises. Heaps of humans in tears with none so poor as to own them as human. They are only national budgetary provisions, not State compassion!

Women are not non-persons, but prisons and semi-prisons have a different version. One ombudsmanic proposal to remedy this jail malady is the involvement of the Social Welfare Department, the Social Welfare Board and other social action groups in the field, together with an effective Watch-Dog Committee with leading, caring persons. That may go a long way to eliminate some of the obvious flaws in the running of these harsh houses.

Punitive warehouses, grumbling women unheeded, cannot be called therapeutic processes. Can't we evolve new institutes where there are no prisoners, only patients? There are no cells, since prisoners are free within the campus, appreciate the affection shown, respond to the drugs given, work to the best of their ability with pride and even earn moderate wages? Self-expression is self-discovery and recovery therapy is creative activity. But where is the wish, the will, the wisdom? Women, after all!

To give her dignity economic, social and personal, is to prepare her to earn a living, not to imprison her for the crime of being poor and trying to survive only mendicancy and flesh market.

Positive, plural proposals to regain women's true dignity and full personality must be executed if elimination of inequality is to be a right in reality. Again, where is the conviction for egalite? Do we take human rights seriously?

Even in civil status and economic affairs, a woman is devalued iniquitously. In family law, she is denied rights similar to the masculine gender. In civil rights and religious functions, she is downgraded. We may generalise that the personality of the disabled gender demands restoration of full opportunity to develop. The Supreme Court, despite constitutional equality of the sexes, has let down, on occasions, the Indian woman, with crude arguments.

At the implementation level, welfare legislations in favour of women meet with their Waterloo. Enforcement is the Achilles' heel of radical law. The truth is that the battle for women's causes is long and hard.

Where are women legislators and law drafters? Where are women judges and magistrates? Where are women police and prosecutors in numbers? Even if a sprinkling of police women are found they are decorative pieces, not even armed? Only a single or perhaps a few police women are a match for men in crime and injustice. Judicial women make only cosmetic presence. So long as the law is a closed male shop, so long as the whole bureaucracy keeps the dice loaded against females, the fatal female destiny will not even be felt, let alone be reversed. Laws may be changed when noises are made, as in the case of penal rape provisions, equal remuneration statutes, anti-dowry anti-sati enactments and so on. But though the Constitution occupies commanding heights, law-in-action is what moulds the rule of life, shapes social justice and makes people feel that courts and prisons are no paper tigers.

Current Currents

Gender Justice, in the Indian context, whatever the resolutions in Constitutions and discussions at international gatherings, has yet to arm the women with the confidence that in this country she matters as a free partner at home, in public places and offices, in opportunities of economic pursuits and social status, in family rights and participation in State processes. True, the battle for Woman Unbound is being waged. Many non-governmental organisations of women have sprung up. Wherever I go, I find women activists in action. Many work among tribals, bonded labourers and construction workers. But sacrificing spirits braving rural adversities are not many. Sincerity there is, spiritual rage there is. However, middle class limitations, familial, social, economic, molestational potential and reputational risks plus sex-related handicaps inhibit the fanning out of women crusaders into hazardous ranges, in awesome urban areas, tribal belts and remote or fundamentalist village environs. That is why the liberal socialite touch in women N.G.O. net work. Splendid workers but urban-based. We have to have rural cadres, tribal cadres, slum cadres, working class cadres. Women turn-out at gender group meetings is encouraging but the meat of the movement is not audience but challenge. For that, activists are visibly absent.

The State is much to blame, and so too all political parties and party-based fronts. No legislation, save one, gives statutory status for women's organisations, on their own, to initiate or intervene in women-related legal proceedings. Indeed, discrimination between officially recognised and non-recognised organisations is a divisive idea meant to debilitate militant activists. The decorative presence of politically respectable women leaders who make appropriate noises is now permitted. But raw, rugged rural fighters and radical ideologues, with unpolished tongue and unembellished truth, are suspect or suppressed. As of right, womanhood has not registered her statutory presence because for legal action. In political terms and vote power equations, through stratagems and tactics women are kept vivisected so that the *female does not matter. Man* makes policies, *woman* is given permission to speak. In a society of *Sita-Sati* syndrome, 'the undone vast' is a guilty interrogation.

Even existing legislation is skin-deep, not soul-deep. Superficial amendments and enactments—good top-dressing-but, in effect, the prejudiced core is untouched. No women's legislation for equal familial rights. Why? Masculine fundamentalism! The Muslim Women (Protection of Rights on Divorce) Act 1986, where a former young Prime Minister, who oft prated about the 21st century, caved in when 'moulvi' politics scared him into discriminating against that most vulnerable sector, the illiterate, submissive, constantly talaq-threatened Muslim sister. Even progressive organs are subtly hostile. No labour union ever revolted or reported to enforce equal remuneration for equal work by women. No woman union leader or political commander; no woman on the high bench, no women's bloc in the House cutting through party lines to act unitedly on women's issues. Government's bonafides is suspect. Proof—Operation Agnivesh where the government men stopped the anti-sati march into Deoraya village. All legislation relating to women are hypocrisy which pays printed homage to gender justice!

A report on the custodial condition of women, presented several years ago by a Government- appointed Committee is not implemented! Not even a White Paper on State Policy vis a vis women in custody, as recommended in that Report (and draft given), is not carried out. All Reports, where women's lot is the subject, suffer purdah. Even the Left Front radicals of Kerala have not published the Thankamoni report by a Judicial officer where policemen were alleged to have molested rural women in a burst of erotic aggression! Instances abound where Governments have shown unconcern for women's rights and wrongs against women. The strategy for women's development must be shaped to antidote the resistance and reluctance stated above. Otherwise, women's status can never be equal.

Her lot, in Shakespearean diction is: "Fraility, thy name is woman." Shall we suffer this slander of Hitlerite flavour? Even Tennyson's lines echo in Indian culture!

> "Man for the field and woman for the hearth;
> Man for the sword and for the needle she;
> Man with the head and woman with the heart;
> Man to command and woman to obey;
> All else confusion."

We must banish this mysogynist pathology ruling Indian social psychology.

Research Trends

It is heartening that despite this bias, researches are unearthing injustices. At the national level, there is a Delhi- based Centre for Women's Development studies under Ms.Veena Majumdar. So also, under the leadership of Phulrenu Guha a masterly Report of 1974 remains a landmark. There are women's Universities in Bombay, Madras and Andhra Pradesh. Colleges for women's studies exist. A valiant band of ideationally militant though operationally restricted, discussion group of young women are in charge of NIPCD (National Institute of Public Cooperation and Child Development). This organisation is ceaselessly organising seminars, workshops and action-oriented discussions. And now a ubiquitous phenomenon is found: Seminars on Women and Development. Good augury. Although seminars, with official drums, often summon the call girls of the establishment, the current crop of women's seminars is not verbal pyrotechnics but anger and agony and serious business. There is hope. But the key is legal literacy and right-conscious mood, with militant meat served in the suppressed villages where women are pregnant with silent rage. India is where they are. *For they are the humans without rights.*

Kerala has made a humble beginning through a non-governmental voluntary agency called People's Council for Social Justice in educating women in their rights. One of its active projects is Legal Literacy for Women. The response is good but constraints are many. The soil is hospitable because Kerala has a generally higher literacy rate and women's status, as a cultural heritage, is less depressing. Even so, miniscale efforts cannot achieve much. A massive campaign, involving the vast masses of illiterate women, is necessitous all over India. Special focus on harijan -girijan sections, where women are no chattel or beasts of burden, is a first priority. Battle-fit assault on Reaction in Bihar, Madhya Pradesh and Uttar Pradesh for vindication of woman's personality is the desideratum. None of these is in evidence now. Police stations, far from being rescue shelters, are fear-laden spider's webs. Just see. A former Chief Minister, Nandini Satpaty, had to seek the writ of the Supreme Court to keep away from the custodial potential and interrogatory menace of a Bhubaneshwar police house. The Minister for Women's Affairs, Mrs. Margaret Alva—a very sensitive, very realistic, very vocal and very distressed—often complains of the implementational impotence of women—focussed measures. They are the orphans of our corpus juris, the still-borns of our statute book.

In this situation of 'sound and fury' in favour of women 'signifying nothing' to the dalit gender of India, the research priority is first regarding their *right to life in dignity*. Such studies must zero-in on the primitive feudal and underworld regions.

A paradign shift is also needed. Till now, the amorphous areas of women in physical, economic and moral danger, gender discrimination in diverse forms, implementational inaction and legislative—judicial delinquency in cases where women's grievances are sharply focussed—these have been the themes, agitational and other. The model must now shift to the Cinderella among women's causes, viz. the battered, beaten mentally distraught women in rural distances, the adivasis who are bought and sold in weekly fairs and temple festivals, only to end up as slaves in city brothels, and the bonded labourers and wretched construction workers, homeless, unfree, breadless and 'whitherless'. Until the last, the lost and the lowliest are salvaged, India remains unfree.

Secondly, a study of the infra-structural weaknesses with bearing on the failure of women's causes, must fall for research. Thirdly, the composition of such research teams and the promotion of non-governmental (even if anti-governmental) voluntary groups should be fall for examination.

Government is the Establishment. The Establishment is allergic to criticism and radicalism. Therefore, a national autonomous agency needs to be set up. Such a Commission must not be a creature of the Administration, which is politically interested in the fourth world remaining the fourth. A statutory National Commission of Women with democratic representation, pluralist composition and accent on the weakest sector is the present need.[5] Such a commission must have the power to monitor and correct, to investigate and even engage in legal proceedings, ignite legislation and exercise ombudsmanic authority.

A National White Paper on Women is a *must* right now. Words have lost their value. Even legislative deeds are dismissed as gimmick. Therefore, gender democracy with power "for Women, by Women and of Women" is the prescription.

A dialectical study of the strengths and failures of women's development and the retarding forces drives us to the conclusion that Constitutional amendments and pro-women legislations have short mileage if political will is weak. The legislator is less than concerned is clear because the legal provisions with regard to women are riddled with lacunae and do not include Women's organisations from operating the punitive apparatus. Many constraints are built into the legislations which make women feel disillusioned. Social crimes against women, in an era of vociferous defence of women's status, is on the increase.

Legal aid to the poor (women) is more on paper because

women are illiterate, weak, shy and do not have the know-how to reach centres where such aid is offered. The delivery system of justice is grossly inadequate although Women Police Cells (Dec. 1986) set up in Delhi for prompt attention to women's cases has yielded results. Now all the Cells in the districts are functioning and are manned by women officers. The number of complaints dealt with by the District Women Cells show that more and more women are approaching them for help. The Cells are becoming more and more popular day by day.

The following necessary inferences are available. Law cannot do it alone. Legislators are indifferent. Enforcement is a casualty. This must change. Voluntary bodies have no meaningful locus standi inside the Police Station, inside the Court, inside the Legal Aid Board, inside every place where action has to be taken. Mere statistics does not reflect the truth because fear and ignorance and socio-cultural constraints, apart from the inhibitive male attitudes towards women's equality, make remedial jurisprudence a rope of sand.

Final

Indian womanhood must demand economic and social dignity in practical terms and insist that the private sector shall, like the public sector, be bound to respect equality of sexes on pain of the state withdrawing all licences, loans and other facilities. The State shall, through all its processes, compel the private sector to comply with the demands of gender justice. A women's code, declaring that, notwithstanding anything to the contrary in any law, a female person shall enjoy the same status, rights and privileges as her male counter-part in like situations must be your magna carta.

A substantial increase in the emergence of women at all levels in all sectors must be actively promoted by the State so that in the legislative, judicial and executive ranks and echelons, in the professions; in arts and crafts, in education and culture, womanhood shall find expression and unfold its potential to augment the nation's human resources.

An ombudsman or President's commission must be created to invigilate, monitor, audit and report on the disabilities, bottlenecks and obstructive tactics whereby womanhood is denied social justice, and the legislatures must discuss such reports and direct follow-up action.

The women of India, equal in talent and versatility of ability, must come in large numbers in the judiciary, legislature and the civil services and in the technological and industrial departments of national life. The political parties must be persuaded to express consensus on the project.

A women's cell in the Law Commission must be set up consisting of women legal activists with sensitized mental antennae who will take prompt steps to enact or amend laws, rules and orders with a view to actualising women's deliverance.

Women's rights are part of human rights. Gender justice is integral to social justice. A revolutionary perspective which battles against exploitation is the soul of the new offensive for operation women's deliverance. Even causes like prohibition, slum rehabilitation, suppression of immoral traffic, have a woman dimension which must be highlighted. Woman in bondage weeps at the lesser levels. Our action, with all its hopes and all its boasts, can never really be free until the last and the least woman among us is free. Therefore, harken to the summons of 'women unbound' and collectively inaugurate this adventure - destination deliverance through operation gender justice. It is a human cause, not a woman's cause. So all activist humans must become a catalyst in the extinguishment of exploitation of our sisters.

Brave new Bharat must make every woman free spiritually, socially, economically, culturally and politically. Such is the imperative of our independence; such is the commitment to the Constitution. Freedom is indivisible as between man and woman. Either both or neither. So woman power shall break its promethean chains and emerge unbound; through law if possible; against the law if necessary.

An Afterword

The International Year and Decade of Women have come and gone but the status of women remains rather static. India, with its shocking *sati*, child marriage, dowry and devadasi praxis, is half-wake but more than half-asleep on issues of women. There is dynamic paper work but, paper-logging is the device of Secretariat engineering to block action. Thus the first comprehensive Report on the Status of Women to the last Report on Custodial Justice to Women and other valuable inquiries, studies, seminars and allied exercises notwithstanding, 'the petty done, the undone vast' stares womanhood in the face. In the cities, foeticide is lucrative medical practice; in the country-side, herbal powder mixed with mother's milk is administered, when the baby at birth is identified as girl, to put it to rest instantly and for ever. Mother's milk not for the life of the child but for its death! This happens today! Infanticide to 'sati'cide, dowry deaths to markets for tribal belles to gang rapes still exist in Gandhi's country! Muslim women themselves, in Parliament's mysterious wisdom, are segregated for purposes of bare maintenance of destitute divorcees! Illiteracy of *women* is double that of men, and economically and socially they are still backward. How many trade unions have women at the top? Legislators from this gender are fewer and Cabinet membership is almost illusory. Even Panchayats do not reflect women's presence, except as tokenism omitting the reservation of seats suddenly trumpeted about in the controversial, dubious Panchayat project in the womb! Lands do not belong to them, authority at home is not her cup of tea. All the humbler chores are hers, and developmentally she is a Cinderalla. Of course, she has the vote and constitutional equality but in reality gender justice is allergy for the Executive, the Legislature and the Judiciary.

Never-the-less, omens of awakening are seen. The dawn is drawing near. But catalytic action is needed to accelerate the process. Andhra Pradesh has given the women coparcenery right. Tamil Nadu proposes to grant it; Women police are being recruited although shamefully low in numbers, status and other conditions and facilities. The gender role in the State process is gradually rising, leaving miles to go, though.

Women's seminars and like phenomena are everywhere and participants, though not from the masses and the marginalised sectors, are sincere and committed, not the call girls of the establishment. But concrete action is still a scarce commodity. Just take the case of the Report on Women in Custody. Over five years have elapsed and most of the recommendations do not involve, for implementation, even a rupee. And yet, departments are dawdling, displaying little concern and inter-ministerial disagreements. Likewise, the Family Courts Act passed years ago has ignited little action. Implementation is the Achelles' heel of women-related reports and legislations.

The new awareness must be intensified and pressure mounted on State and Central Governments so that gender justice may be accelerated. Where there is inaction, delinquency or violation of laws and orders, a monitoring machinery and administrative/ legal process may have to be innovated so that quick correctional measures may be undertaken by an appropriate authority clothed with adequate powers. Periodic survey of progress and shortfall, proposals for changes, further legal proceedings and so on may be taken by that Gender Ombudsman. A statutory Commission, like the S.C./S.T. Commission under the Constitution, together with wider powers of correction and sanction against deviance, not mere reporting of failures, nor recommendations of changes —that is the minimum functionalism to push the case for womanhood's rights into socio-economic and legal locomotion.

Some legislation at the Central and State levels exists in theory but, in fact, is moribund. Even as I write these lines I hear the holy chants of Puthrakameshti Yaga in the neighbouring shrine. Scriptures are uttered, pujas are performed, money flows in holy incense and the police keep watch all round against women protesters. The entire Operation Yajna is to win the birth of a Male Child invoking God's powers for the discriminatory achievement of Boy Child! A girl is unwanted; and in India of the 21st century she is still a slave if born and survives.

In the Christian community equal inheritance was denied to the daughter in Travancore and Cochin despite Constitutional rhetoric of equality in sex. Where job avenues exist there is a subtle exclusion of women even for journalists' posts. On enquiry, one gathers that this rejection of women applicants is because they claim facilities for maternity leave and nocturnal protection. The masculine culture fails to understand that the woman has to undergo all the ordeals of pregnancy, child birth, upbringing and what not so that the human species may survive and civilization may advance. This social blessing which humanity derives from womanhood is forgotten when men, as the bosses of economic enterprises, refuse to accept on equal terms girls who apply for posts even though they are well qualified. Alas, prejudices die hard.

Two ideas must invigorate the mass upsurge required at the present juncture when the woman question is coming of age.

Ideologically, what is demanded is more than mere economic subsistence, more than bare equality, more than liberation in familial, religious and other spheres. It is the uninhibited *right to be oneself* and the equal opportunity to develop oneself as one decides, not as the masculine-dominated mandate or community's male ethos prescribes or proscribes.

The princess may be above personal want but is only a dainty doll; the slum woman has to do every chore all through the day and be a tortured slave. Some job, with husband's or parent's goodwill, is not the goal. She must fashion her career by choice and unfold her personality by right. Biological differences there are, but equal freedom will obliterate gender discrimination.

Even the argument that family is the sacred unit and the woman has special obligation in the family cannot but be rejected because this is only crypto-Hitler commandment to keep the woman, serf-like housewife. In this 'family unit' theory is a specious plea to justify unpaid female bonded labour.

Cooking is woman's burden, home her workhouse, fuel collection is woman's task, drinking water carrying is also her job. Looking after children, sending them to school, taking care of their food and health and doing the menial jobs in the home are her responsibility. Why should it be? Sharing and caring is gender justice.

A radical rejection of the repression Ibsen projects is the cry of the woman :

> There are two kinds of moral law, two kinds of consciences, in men and women, and they are altogether different. The two sexes do not understand each other. But in practical life, the woman is judged by man's law, as if she were a man, not a woman.

A series of conventions, instruments and constitutional provisions and world meets bringing women everywhere to come together to launch the new offensive for dynamic gender justice are currently weaving a Woman Power Movement. Women of the World Unite! You have nothing to lose except your chains. You have your whole personhood to gain. This indivisibility of Gender Freedom and the will to radical rupture with traditional culture must fire the drive to Destination Sex Justice.

NOTES AND REFERENCES

1. Women's Rights Conventions, Manifesto, Seneca Falls, 1848.
2. The United Nations and Human Rights, United Nations, New York, p. 148 (1984).
3. *Ibid*. pp. 148-149.
4. *Id*. at 175.
5. A National Commission for Women has been set up in 1992, under the National Commission for Women Act, 1990.

MONOGAMY IN INDIA

*V.S. Deshpande**

Among the Hindus and the Muslims polygamy had been legal. But the Hindu Marriage Act, 1955 has imposed monogamy on Hindus. Thereafter it is only the Muslim community which is not monogamous. The Hindus, Christians and Parsees are made monogamous. There are thus two sets of laws. On the one hand, there are the laws imposing monogamy on the Hindus, Christians and Parsees. On the other hand, there is the personal law of the Muslims which permits polygamy. This is obviously discriminatory.

Articles 14 and 15(1) of the Constitution are Contravened

Article 14 of the Constitution lays down the broad principle that "the State shall not deny to any person equality before the law or the equal protection of the laws within the territory of India".

Article 15(1) more specifically states that "the State shall not discriminate against any citizen on grounds only of religion, race, caste, sex, place of birth or any of them".

The striking thing which emerges out of the above legal situation is this. Polyandry, meaning a woman marrying more than one husband is not allowed in India. Polygamy meaning a man marrying more than one wife is allowed among the Muslims by the Muslim personal law. This leads to discrimination, firstly, against Muslim women. A Muslim woman merely because she is a Muslim by religion is denied monogamy by her personal law while women belonging to other religious communities are given the benefit of monogamy by the statutes governing them. Secondly, this has led to discrimination even against women of

* Former Chief Justice, Delhi High Court, New Delhi.

other religious communities. This is because a Hindu or a Christian husband who cannot marry a second wife can convert himself to Islam merely for the purpose of marrying a second wife on the ground that after his conversion he is governed by the Muslim personal law and thereunder he can marry more than one wives.

The prohibition of discrimination by the State in Articles 14 and 15(1) applies not only to executive action of the State but also to legislative action of the State. This is why Article 13 declares any law contrary to the Constitution as invalid. The definition of "Law" in Article 13 is only inclusive and, therefore, the word "law" is to be construed to include all law which is enforced by the State. Therefore, the Muslim personal law in so far as it is enforced by the State is "law" and would be unconstitutional if it is discriminatory, particularly because the discrimination is based, firstly, on religion and, secondly, on sex contrary to Article 15(1).

Fraud on the Law

Such conversions are a fraud on the law. These husbands by such conversions are not exercising their fundamental right to freedom of religion guaranteed by Article 25 of the Constitution. That right is called "freedom of conscience and free profession, practice and propagation of religion". That right presupposes a belief in the religion concerned. But the Hindu or the Christian husband who becomes a Muslim merely for the purpose of marrying a second wife is obviously not interested in Islam as a religion. He is merely trying to take advantage of the Muslim personal law to defeat the monogamy imposed by the laws governing the Hindus and the Christians. Islam is a noble religion as all religions are noble. It could not be the intention of Islam to lure Hindu and Christian husbands to Islam merely for the purpose of marrying a second wife even though such husbands may not have any belief in Islam. Muslim personal law cannot, therefore, be presumed to apply to permit such a fraudulent convert to Islam to marry a second wife.

Such fraudulent use of law is not permissible. The fraudulent use of the Muslim personal law to defeat the monogamy imposed by the Hindu Marriage Act, 1955 takes place due to the existence of two parallel laws, namely the Muslim Personal Law and the Hindu Law existing side by side. A similar situation exists in the field of conflict of laws. Two legal systems governing two countries may exist side by side. Can a person take advantage of one legal system to defeat the other legal system? This question arose in *Smt. Satya* v. *Teja Singh*.[1] The husband governed by the Hindu law purported to be domiciled in the State of Nevada in the U.S.A. thus giving jurisdiction to the court in Nevada to entertain the petition of divorce against his wife in Nevada. He obtained a decree against her from Nevada court. When his wife sued him for maintenance in India, the question arose whether the husband was liable to pay maintenance or whether he was not so liable because the marriage had been dissolved by the court in Nevada, U.S.A. The Supreme Court in para 18 of the judgement observed as follows:

> In determining whether a divorce decree will be recognised in another jurisdiction as a matter of comity, public policy and good morals may be considered. No country is bound by comity to give effect in its courts to divorce laws of another country which are repugnant to its own laws and public policy. Thus, where a "mail-order divorce" granted by a Mexican court was not based on jurisdictional finding of domicile, the decree was held to have no extraterritorial effect in New Jersey (*State* v. *Najjar* 2 NJ 208). American courts generally abhor the collusive Mexican mail-order divorces and refuse to recognize them (*Langner* v. *Langner* 39 NYS 2d 918). Mail-order divorces are obtained by correspondence by a spouse not domiciled in Mexico. Latey, in his well-known book on divorce says that "The facilities afforded by the Mexican courts to grant divorces to all and sundry whatsoever their nationality or domicile have become even more notorious than those in Reno, Nevada." Recognition is denied to such decrees as a matter of public policy.

In para 21 the Court says:

> A foreign decree of divorce is subjected to collateral attack for fraud or for want of jurisdiction either of the subject-matter or of the parties provided that the attacking party is not estopped from doing so (*Cohen* v. *Randall* 1943-86 Law-

> yers ed 480). A foreign decree of divorce obtained by fraud is void. *Fraudulent simulation of domicile is impermissible.* A spouse who goes to a State or country other than that of the matrimonial domicile for the sole purpose of obtaining a divorce perpetrates a fraud, and the judgement is not binding on the courts of other States.

The doctrine of fraud on a statute or a fraud on a law is fully brought out by the analogy of the conflict of laws cited above. Domicile under the law of a legal system may be obtained by a stay in the country of the legal system for a certain period of time. Nevertheless, if a person does not really wish to stay in that country but stays there merely for the purpose of obtaining domicile to use the domicile only for the purpose of getting a divorce and not for the purpose of staying in the State then such domicile though literally satisfying the law, is a fraud on that law and would not, therefore, be recognized by another legal system which is also defrauded by such action.

The analogy of this principle in conflict of laws is very close to the analogy of a husband converting himself to Islam, not because he believes in Islam but merely to commit a fraud on the Muslim Personal Law and also on the Hindu Marriage Act to marry a second wife.

In para 40 of the judgment the Supreme Court said:

> The recital in the judgment of the Nevada court that the respondent was a bona fide resident of and was domiciled in Nevada is not conclusive and can be contradicted by satisfactory proof.

That is to say, it could be shown that the residence of the person was not bonafide but was merely to claim domicile to achieve the purpose of divorce.

In para 45 of the judgment the Court further says:

> But residence for a particular purpose fails to answer the qualitative test, for, the purpose being accomplished the residence would cease. The residence must answer "a qualitative as well as a quantitative test," that is, the two elements of *factum* and *animus* must concur. The respondent went to Nevada forum-hunting, found a convenient jurisdiction which

would easily purvey a divorce to him and left it even before the ink on his domiciliary assertion was dry. Thus, the decree of the Nevada court lacks jurisdiction. It can receive no recognition in our courts.

Qualitative Test

The important distinction made by the Supreme Court above is to impose a qualitative test over and above the quantitative test. Acquisition of domicile is not to be made merely by a literal compliance with the stay in a particular country for the required period of time. Such residence must also be accompanied by an intention to stay permanently in that country. The very meaning of domicile is the intention to stay indefinitely in a country. Therefore, a stay, even if it is for the requisite period, but is not with an intention to stay there permanently, does not satisfy the qualitative test of the respondent even if it satisfies the quantitative tests.

In the same way, the conversion of a Hindu or a Christian husband to Islam may satisfy the factual requirements, but since the only reason why the conversion was undertaken was to marry a second wife such conversion is not to be regarded as genuine. Afterall belief in a religion is a noble sentiment and a matter of the spirit. When a true belief in the religion is wanting, merely complying with the formalities of conversion would not make the convert belong to the new religion. The qualitative test will not be satisfied.

The jurisdiction of the Nevada court was denied only because the domicile obtained by the husband was not genuine. The husband did not intend to stay in Nevada permanently. He went there only to obtain the domicile to divorce his wife in India.

Indeed, the genuineness of a conversion has been held to be a matter into which the courts can enquire.[2]

Public Policy

Section 23 of the Contract Act says that a contract which is opposed to public policy is void. The principle was extended to a divorce in *Joao Gloria Pires* v. *Ana Joaquina Rodrigues e Pires and another*.[3] In that case a Roman Catholic marriage had been solemnized in Goa. The husband later on secured a divorce decree from a foreign court. But the Division Bench of the Judicial Commissioners Court in Goa held in this case that the divorce decree could not be recognized because a Catholic marriage is indissoluble. The divorce was thus against public policy as stated in Section 23 of the Contract Act. Indeed, the Court referred to Cheshire on the *Principles of Private International Law* and his description of limping marriages. A limping marriage means a marriage recognized in one country but not in another country. Applying this analogy to the case of conversion it would mean that even if the Muslim Personal Law were to recognize the conversion of a Hindu or a Christian husband to Islam as valid, the Hindu and the Christian personal laws may not recognize it as valid. Like a limping marriage this would be a limping conversion.

The significance of public policy must be realized as a distinct ground. One ground to deny validity to the conversion is because the conversion is not genuine and is intended to be a fraud both on the Muslim laws as also on the Hindu and Christian personal laws. But even if it is assumed that the Muslim law will recognize such a conversion, it may still not be recognized by the Hindu and the Christian personal laws on the ground that such a conversion is opposed to public policy.

Overriding Grounds

The grounds of fraud on the law and contravention of public policy are overriding grounds in the sense that they will deny effect to a conversion of a Hindu or a Christian husband to Islam merely for the purpose of marrying a second wife even if on a literal interpretation the Hindu Marriage Act may not be contravened by a conversion to Islam. A mechanical view of the Hindu Marriage Act would not defeat the fraud on the law resulting from such conversion. For, the monogamy imposed by Section 5 of the Hindu Marriage Act is on two Hindus entering into marriage. If the husband is no longer a Hindu when he marries a second wife then the prohibition by Section 5(1) may not apply.

Similarly, Section 17 of the Hindu Marriage Act prohibits bigamy only when "any marriage between two Hindus solemnized after the commencement of this Act is void if at the date of such marriage either party had a husband or wife living". Again, it would be argued that the husband was not a Hindu when he married a second wife and is not, therefore, within the mischief of Section 17.

But the Christian Marriage Act is different. Section 4 of the Indian Christian Marriage Act 1872 applies to every marriage between persons "one or both of whom is or are a Christian."

Section 60(2) of the Christian Marriage act requires that neither of the persons intending to be married shall have a wife or husband still living. The marriage to be solemnised under the Act is a marriage between one or both parties being a Christian. Since the Act applies even if one of the parties is a Christian, Section 4 would continue to apply to a Christian husband even after his conversion. In this respect it is to be contrasted with Section 5 of the Hindu Marriage Act which restricts a Hindu marriage as being between two Hindus. It is arguable, therefore, that a Christian marriage will govern the rights of a husband even if he is converted to Islam and will prohibit his marriage with a second wife. The Parsi Marriage and Divorce Act, 1936 is, however, proof against conversion to Islam. Section 4 specifically prohibits remarriage in the following words:

> Section 4(1) — No Parsi (whether such Parsi has changed his or her religion or domicile or not) shall contract any marriage under this Act or any other law in the lifetime of his or her wife or husband, whether a Parsi or not, except after his or her lawful divorce from such wife or husband. . . .
>
> Section 4(2) —Every marriage contracted contrary to the provisions of sub-section (1) shall be void.

Shariat Act, 1937

Any doubt which may exist regarding the enforcement of the Muslim personal law as being State action contrary to Articles 13, 14 and 15(1) of the Constitution would be removed by the Muslim personal law (*Shariat*) Application Act, 1937. Section 2 of this Act says:

> Notwithstanding any customs or usage to the contrary, in all questions regarding . . . marriage, dissolution of marriage . . . in cases where the parties are Muslims shall be the Muslim personal law (*Shariat*).

This is a statute and, therefore, the marriage of two Muslims is after this Act governed by the Shariat Act and not by the uncodified Muslim Personal Law. There can be no doubt that when a Hindu husband converted to Islam marries a non-Muslim woman that marriage will not be governed by the Shariat Act since both the parties to the marriage would not be Muslims. The Muslim personal law will not, therefore, validate such marriage. Most of such converts do not even change their names after conversion and marry another woman in the Hindu community itself in the majority of cases. Such a second marriage will not be saved by the Muslim personal law in view of the Shariat Act, 1937.

Muslim Personal Law is not Religion

The question whether Muslim personal law is religion is answered by the Constitution itself. Firstly, statutes have been enacted to change the Muslim personal law such as the Shariat Act, 1937 and the Dissolution of Muslim Marriage Act, 1939. Secondly Entry 5 in the Concurrent List of the VII Schedule to the Constitution expressly enables both the Central and the State Legislatures to make laws regarding "marriage and divorce . . .; all matters in respect of which parties in judicial proceeding were immediately before the commencement of this Constitution subject to their personal law."

This is, therefore, an express constitutional provision putting it beyond doubt that marriage under the personal laws is not religion but is a subject on which legislation can be made and has been made by the State. There can be no doubt, therefore, that the Muslim marriage law is enforced by State action and not by Islam as a religion. There would, therefore, be no contravention of Islam if the Muslim marriage law in this respect is held to be unconstitutional by the courts being discriminatory.

Genuineness of Conversion

The genuineness of a conversion from one religion to another in India should be a justiciable issue. The analogy of the genuineness of a domicile considered and decided in *Satya*[4] should be followed. The justiciability would be based on treating the personal law created by adherence to a religion to be on the same footing as a personal law attaching to a person by reason of his domicile. The word "personal law" was used in this sense by Dicey & Morris in Rule 37 of their book *Conflict of Laws*, 10th edition. Rule 37 was framed as follows:

> A man or a woman whose personal law does not permit polygamy has no capacity to contract a valid polygamous marriage.

Just as a marriage celebrated between persons governed by a monogamous law of their domicile cannot be later governed by a polygamous law unless a party changes his or her domicile and adopts a polygamous law of the new domicile, similarly a marriage between persons governed by a monogamous personal law of their religion cannot be made polygamous unless the husband converts himself to Islam which alone permits polygamy to Muslim men. The analogy of the personal law of domicile with the personal law of religion is thus complete. The authority for considering and deciding upon the genuineness of the conversion would be the same as the authority for considering and deciding the genuineness of a domicile. *Satya* decided by the Supreme Court as above is that authority.

Conflict of Personal Laws

Just as the branch of law called conflict of laws has developed as a system of national law, inter alia, to determine the applicability of a national law on a subject involving a foreign element, the same branch of law called the conflict of laws has also to be applied when the laws of different communities inside a country differ from each other. For instance, in India the Hindus, Muslims and Christians are governed by their different personal laws. They differ from each other. Normally, parties belonging to these religious communities are governed exclusively by the personal law of each of them, but there may be a matter in which two parties belonging to two different religious communities are involved and the question arises as to which personal law would apply. In that event, it would be logical to apply the principles of conflict of laws. For, the essence of the conflict of laws is that the two parties are governed by different systems of law. It is immaterial whether these systems are of national laws or they are personal laws inside one country.

In the following decisions conflict of laws principles were applied to such questions arising between two parties governed by different personal laws inside India. In *Sayyeda Khatoon* v. *Ovedia*[5] two Jews domiciled in India performed their marriage in India in 1943 by Jewish ceremonies. In 1945 the wife embraced Islam and offered it to her husband. On his refusal to accept it she launched divorce proceedings. Dismissing the petition, the Court observed that there was no law under which a marriage performed under one personal law could be dissolved under another personal law just because one of the parties has converted to another religion. This decision is logical because it is in accordance with the principles of conflict of laws as applied to different national systems of law. If, therefore, a Hindu marriage between two Hindus is governed by Section 5(i) insisting on monogamy then Section 17 of the same Act would make a perfect sense. It is because the marriage under Section 5(i) has been a monogamous marriage between two Hindus that, according to Section 17, "any marriage between two Hindus solemnized after the commencement of this Act is void if at the date of such marriage either party had a husband or wife living; and the provisions of Sections 494 and 495 of the Indian Penal Code shall apply accordingly". The whole of the Act has to be read together as forming one scheme. Obviously, Section 17 can apply only when the earlier marriage was between two Hindus which had to be monogamous under the Act. It is only if the earlier marriage was between a Muslim husband and a Hindu wife that Section 17 would not apply because the earlier marriage itself would permit polygamy to the husband. This is not expressly stated but is necessarily implied in Section 17.

Otherwise, it would not make sense. Vice versa, if in the earlier marriage the parties were Hindus and therefore monogamous then any subsequent marriage between either of the parties to the earlier marriage would be void because of the monogamy imposed by the earlier marriage. When the later marriage between two Hindus, one of whom was a party to the earlier marriage, is declared void it is because of the monogamy which is attached to each of the parties of the earlier marriage by virtue of the earlier monogamous marriage governed by the Hindu personal law. It could not be the intention of Sections 5(i) and 17 to permit an easy evasion of monogamy imposed by an earlier marriage by allowing the husband to the earlier marriage to become a Muslim and marry a second wife and thereby avoiding the consequences of Section 17.

This interpretation is supported by Section 13(1)(ii) of the same Act. It says: "Any marriage solemnized, whether before or after the commencement of this Act, may, on a petition presented by either the husband or the wife, be dissolved by a decree of divorce on the ground that the other party has after the solemnization of the marriage, . . . has ceased to be a Hindu by conversion to another religion". This ground of divorce can be fully understood only when it is presumed that the marriage sought to be dissolved is a monogamous marriage. This is why the wife is not made to tolerate the conversion of the husband to another religion. Divorce is also sought under a provision of the Hindu Marriage Act which applies only to Hindus. The other relevant sections, namely 5 and 17 also apply to Hindus only. If Section 13(1)(ii) has to apply to a Hindu and another party belonging to another religion then the implication is that the conversion of the other party to another religion is not regarded as coming in the way of application of Section 13 of the Hindu Marriage Act to the suit for dissolution of marriage by divorce. If the conversion is disregarded for the purpose of applying Section 13, then it can also be disregarded for the purpose of the application of Section 17. That is the only logical meaning to be given to Section 17. Otherwise Section 17 can be made meaningless if it is not to be applied because the second marriage by the husband is after conversion to Islam.

The view expressed in *Sayyeda Khatoon*[6] that a marriage performed under one personal law could not be dissolved under another personal law can also lead to the principle that a marriage performed under the monogamous Hindu law cannot be evaded by conversion to Islam. The view expressed in this case was also the view taken in two subsequent decisions, namely *Rakeya Bibi*[7] and *Rabav Khanan* v. *Khodadad*.[8]

A Harmony of Laws

However, the necessity to hold that either the Shariat Act or the Muslim personal law is unconstitutional being discriminatory will be dispensed with if the Muslim personal law is interpreted reasonably and a fraudulant conversion undertaken only to defeat monogamy imposed by the Hindu law is not recognized as a genuine conversion to Islam. In that event the Hindu husband converted to Islam would continue to be governed by the Hindu Marriage Act as still a Hindu and would not be able to marry a second wife. This is what I had pleaded in the keynote address at the All-India Seminar on Women and the Law on 17-18 October, 1981.[9] Unfortunately, too many conversions of Hindu husbands which are patently fraudulent are taking place every day and such converts are marrying second wives with impunity. This has made the Hindu Marriage Act ineffective in this respect. It has also deprived Hindu women of the protection of law. It has further held out a very unwholesome example of fraud on the law which is demoralizing to the Indian society as a whole including all the religious communities. In the whole world such an instance of monogamy being defeated by such a trick will not be found. The Indian situation is, therefore, intolerable and needs an immediate decision by the Supreme Court or a legislation by Parliament. The preferable solution, of course, would be the decision of a court declaring the second marriage of a converted Hindu husband as void because the conversion is not genuine. This will continue the harmony among the different personal laws and will not necessitate a decision whether the Muslim personal law is discriminatory or not.

NOTES AND REFERENCES

1. AIR 1975 S.C. 105.
2. *Rakeya Bibi* v. *Anil Kumar*, ILR (1948) 2 Cal. 119.
3. AIR 1967 Goa, 113.
4. *Supra* note 1.
5. (1945) 49 CWH 754.
6. *Ibid.*
7. *Supra* note 2.
8. AIR 1947 Bom. 272.
9. AIR 1982, Journal section, p. 1.

FAMILY COURTS : SOME REFLECTIONS

*P.M. Bakshi**

Family Courts are being established all over India. The time has come to deal with some important aspects. The present article deals with certain procedural aspects.

Procedure, and the Judge's Role in Trial and Settlement

Efforts at Settlement

It is a recurring theme of the modern approach to family law, that there should be efforts at settlement. This aspect was emphasised positively by the Law Commission which, when revising the Code of Civil Procedure, 1908, recommended the insertion of Order 32A, which recommendation has now been implemented. Order 32A was inserted in the Code to set out a comprehensive group of provisions, incorporating several facets of the proper approach to be adopted by the judiciary in regard to disputes concerning the family. One of the provisions in that Order highlights the duty of the court to make efforts at settlement. This emphasis, suggested by the Law Commission of India, has been repeated by the Legislature in Family Courts Act, 1984, sections 9, 10(3), 21(2)(c) etc. Taken together, section 9(1) and 9(2) will be found to yield four important propositions as under :

(i) The Family Court shall, in the first instance (consistently with the nature and circumstances of the case) make an endeavour to assist and persuade the parties in arriving at a settlement.

(ii) For this purpose, the Family Court may follow such procedure as it thinks fit. This proposition is laid down in section 9(1), latter half, and repeated in section 10(3).

* Director, Indian Law Institute, New Delhi

(iii) Where, in a particular State, the High Court has made any rules as to the procedure to be followed in assisting and persuading the parties in arriving at a settlement, those rules are to be observed. This proposition is laid down in section 9(1), latter half and repeated (indirectly) in section 21(2)(c), which gives the High Court power to make rules as to the procedure to be followed in effecting settlement.

(iv) If there is a reasonable possibility of settlement, the Family Court may adjourn the proceeding to enable such efforts to be made, as provided in section 9(2). Of course, section 9(3) makes it clear that this does not affect any other power of the Family Court to adjourn the proceedings. It may incidentally be noted that such power is conferred on every civil court by Order 17, rule 1, Code of Civil Procedure, 1908 which applies to a Family Court by virtue of section 10(1), Family Courts Act. A substantially similar provision is to be found in the Code of Criminal Procedure, 1973, which applies to a Family Court when it tries applications for maintenance under section 125 of that Code as provided in section 10(2), Family Courts Act.

(v) Finally, it may be mentioned that provisions contained in sections 5, 6(1) and 12 of the Family Courts Act, for the association or appointment of Counsellors, welfare officers and welfare agencies are intended, *inter alia*, to facilitate the discharge, by the Family Court, of its duty to promote settlement.

At the same time, it must be pointed out that once the matter goes to the Court, the parties are not in frame of mind to agree to a settlement. The seeds of disharmony would have been sown, long before litigation commenced. The real need is to have adequate counselling services available at that time. Of course, this is not a matter of legislation. It is a need that can be fulfilled, only when we can provide sufficient number of counsellors, whose services can be availed of by married couples in whose life, signs of tension have begun to appear. To reach such a stage, we need not only an augmentation of training courses for the purpose, but also repeated and sustained efforts at keeping the persons so engaged in gainful employment. The employment should be such that the training which they might have received, can be properly utilised. It is further to be pointed out that marital and family counselling appears to be a specialised branch of counselling in general and may, accordingly, need a high expertise.

Though primarily this is a matter of extra-legal action, it would be better if the Family Courts Act, 1984 also contained a provision on the subject, say, as section 6A, somewhat on the following lines :

"6A. Duty of the State Government regarding counselling institutions.—It shall be the duty of the State Government—

(a) to make endeavour to create and maintain, or assist in the creation or maintenance of, institutions engaged in the training of persons in counselling and conciliation in matters concerning the family;

(b) to promote research in, and study of, techniques of such counselling and conciliation, and to disseminate the results of such research and study; and

(c) to give proper publicity to the work done by, and the availability of, institutions which offer counselling and conciliation services in matters concerning the family".

In the context of counselling services, one more aspect deserves consideration. At present, the Act seems to give predominance to officials as counsellors—sections 6 and 23(2)(b). No doubt, the Act does not totally rule out non-official counsellors, as is apparent from sections 5, 12 and 23(2)(c). Still, there seems to be need for drawing attention to the possibility of "associating" non-official counsellors more actively with Family Courts. It is understood that such an experiment was made a few years ago in the City Civil Court, Bombay and was found to be fairly successful. The counsellors who were attached to that court (in its jurisdiction on the matrimonial side) were persons belonging to the Tata Institute of Social Sciences; and it is understood that they did excellent work. Such experiments need to be followed elsewhere also.

Procedure Generally : Section 10

The procedure of Family Courts is governed by section 10, of the Act. This is linked with the jurisdiction exercisable by the Family Courts. Under section 7, the Court exercises two types of jurisdiction, namely—

(a) the jurisdiction exercisable by civil courts in respect of the suit and proceedings enumerated in section 7(1), Explanation; and

(b) the jurisdiction exercisable by magistrates under section 125, Code of Criminal Procedure, 1973 in respect of proceedings for maintenance.

As regards jurisdiction falling in category (a) above, the Family Courts Act, in section 10(1), provides that the Code of Civil Procedure, 1908 shall apply. However, this is subject to the provisions of the Family Courts Act itself and the rules made under that Act. Such rule-making power is conferred –

(i) on the High Courts, by section 21(1) and section 21(2)(c); and

(ii) on the State Government, by sections 5 and 23.

As regards category (b) above, section 10(2) of the Family Courts Act provides that the Code of Criminal Procedure, 1973 and the rules made thereunder shall apply to such proceedings. But this is also subject to the provisions of the Family Courts Act itself and the rules made thereunder.

Special Powers of Family Courts

The applicability of the two Procedural Codes to Family Courts by virtue of the provisions discussed in the preceding paragraph is subject to an important provision contained in section 10(3) of the Family Courts Act, which reads as under :

"(3) Nothing in sub-section (1) or sub-section (2) shall prevent a Family Court from laying down its own procedure with a view to arrive at a settlement in respect of the subject matter of the suit or proceeding, or at the truth of the facts alleged by one party and denied by the other."

This sub-section can prove to be a highly potent weapon in the hands of the Family Court. While it does not seem to give a blank cheque to the Family Court to disregard or override the Family Courts Act or rules made thereunder, it does contemplate that in order to achieve the twin objectives mentioned therein, the Family Court may take procedural action which may be beyond the terms of the respective Codes and (probably), not strictly consistent with the letter of the provisions of the two Codes.

It is in this context that the twin objectives mentioned in section 10(3) need to be analysed. For the sake of convenience, these objectives may be re-stated in brief as –

(i) the objective of arriving at a settlement; and
(ii) the objective of arriving at the truth of the facts in issue.

As regards objective (i) above, the promotion of settlement between the parties, (which is a recurrent theme under sections 5, 6, 9, 12 and 21(2)(c)), may justify the Family Court in playing a more active part in the process of settlement, than it would be able to play in a trial before an ordinary civil court not governed by the Family Courts Act. For this purpose, the important words of section 10(3) are—"laying down its own procedure." The language used is not merely *"adopting or following* its own procedure", but *"laying down* its own procedure." This may be contrasted with section 9(1). On the wording of section 10(3), it would appear that if the Family Court proposes to embark on a particular course of action, it will have to give reasonable notice to the parties, of its proposal. In fact, it can be suggested without impropriety that if the details of the very procedure for settlement are decided by the Family Court in consultation with the parties, such consultation may be conducive to a smooth and speedy settlement in the end.

One more point may be made regarding procedure. A Family Court is authorised "to lay down its own procedure." This means, that there will be an element of individual approach in each Family Court; and it is conceivable that the approach may differ from one judge to another. In fact, it is conceivable, that the approach adopted by a particular judge in one case may differ from the approach to be adopted by him in another case. It appears to be the inarticulate major premise of section 10(3), that in arriving at a settlement, the personality of the judge should be allowed its full play. Reasonable elasticity is the hallmark of the procedure contemplated by section 10(3).

One must now turn to the second objective referred to section 10(3), which is that of arriving at the truth of the facts alleged by one party and denied by the other. Section 10(3), (so far as is material), provides that nothing in the two Codes shall prevent the Family Court from laying down its own procedure in arriving at the truth. Although apparently simple, this provision is likely to lead to a number of questions being raised in practice in due course when occasion arises. What should be the role precisely to be played by the judge in this regard? It is likely that in answering this question, three rival interpretations will be advanced as under :

(i) The presiding judge must make his own efforts at finding out the truth and he must, for that purpose, himself take the initiative, without depending on the parties and must actively conduct the trial.

(ii) While the presiding judge is not expected to investigate the facts on his own initiative, nor to participate actively in the trial in the first instance, yet, if the conduct of the trial by the parties leaves some gaps or obscurities or conflicts or inconsistencies in respect of essential facts in the end, the judge *should* make his own efforts to ascertain the truth. This is a milder interpretation than (i) above.

(iii) If the conduct of the trial by the parties leaves some gaps or obscurities or conflicts or inconsistencies about essential facts in the end, then the presiding judge *may* (though he is not bound to) ascertain the truth. This interpretation is milder than the interpretations at (i) and (ii) above.

It will be noticed that the first interpretation suggested above in respect of the relevant words of section 10(3), Family Courts Act, places the role of the judge at the highest and he would practically come to occupy the centre of the stage at the trial. The second interpretation suggested above does not place him so high, but this interpretation still constitutes an important departure from the normal role of the judge in a civil trial. The third interpretation suggested above is a modified version of the second in as much as the judge is *permitted*, but not required, to make his own efforts to ascertain the truth—in either case, first allowing the parties to take their own initiative.

It is submitted that the language of section 10(3) does not go so far, as to justify the first interpretation. The sub-section begins with the words "Nothing . . . shall prevent a Family Court from laying down its own procedure." The liberty of the presiding judge is saved by these words, but they do not seem to contemplate that, *from the beginning*, he must undertake the role of an investigator into truth. In other words, the language does not contemplate that the adversary system of trial, which is understood to be an essential part of the Indian legal system, should be totally replaced by a "Judge-oriented" system of trial. If that had been the intention, one would have expected more clear and emphatic phraseology in the section. Nor does Order 32A of the Code of Civil Procedure, 1908 (which contains certain special provisions as to suits concerning the family), contemplate such a radical transformation of the role of the judge.

The second interpretation suggested above is also not contemplated by section 10(3). There is no positive or express mandate to the judge. What is preserved is his liberty to follow his own procedure in arriving at the truth. The initial journey must be performed with the help of the parties. Having done so, if the judge finds that he is not able to reach the destination, he is free to take over the direction of the remaining part of the journey, but only in order to arrive at the truth. He is not required in *every case* to follow this course of action, but he is free to do so. It is a discretion and not a duty. Of course, like all discretionary powers of a judge, this also must be exercised judicially. The question may arise as to how far the appellate court will interfere with the discretion. In this connection, the sound view expressed by Lord Justice Davies in *In re O (infant)*, (1971) Ch. 748 : (1971) 2 All E.R. 744 (CA) (an appeal from an order relating to custody) is worth quoting :

> ". . . Every court has a duty to do its best to arrive at a proper and just decision. And if the Appellate Court is satisfied that the decision of the court below is improper, unjust or wrong, then the decision must be set aside. I am quite unable to subscribe to the view that a decision must be treated as sacrosanct because it was made in the exercise of 'discretion'; so to do might well perpetuate injustice."

Even on the mildest interpretation of section 10(3), as suggested above, the provision has considerable utility. As a rule, the two procedural codes in India do not highlight the role of the judge. Though he is permitted to question witnesses in certain cases, in practice, the precise ambit of the relevant provisions remains vague. In any case, they do not confer on the judge a power, in so many words, to make his own efforts to arrive at the truth. Section 10(3) of the Family Courts Act (on this point) makes a *positive* provision, recognising the discretion of the judge. Besides this, sections 5(d), 6(1), 12 and 13 furnish certain mechanisms, facilitating the exercise by the judge of such powers.

Some hypothetical cases can be taken to illustrate the utility of the discretion vested in the presiding judge under section 10(3), "to arrive at the truth"—

(i) A dispute arises about the legitimacy of the child. The rival claimants produce oral evidence, but do not produce any medical evidence in the nature of blood tests or DNA finger prints. In such a case, the judge of the Family Court may get such tests done for arriving at the truth—of course, with the consent of the person concerned.

(ii) There is a dispute as to whether a Shastric marriage ceremony was performed between the parties whose marriage is in dispute. The priest who officiated at the marriage is known and available as a witness, but neither party produces him as a witness. The presiding judge of the Family Court may, in his discretion, summon the priest to record his statement.

(iii) The husband files a petition for divorce, on the ground that he had undergone vasectomy and that the subsequent pregnancy of the wife was through another person. The wife denies that she ever had sexual relations with any other person. The question arises whether the vasectomy had been effectively performed. The judge presiding over the Family Court may summon the hospital records relating to the alleged vasectomy.

These illustrative situations show the utility of the discretion vested in the judge. However, there is one point on which the rule-making section in the Family Courts Act needs amendment. At present, section 21(2)(c) of the Act empowers the High Court to make rules to provide for—

> "(c) the efforts which may be made or the procedure which may be followed by a Family Court for assisting and persuading the parties to arrive at a settlement."

In order to fully implement the intendment of section 10(3), which contemplates efforts by the Family Court, not only towards settlement, but also towards arriving at the truth, it appears to be desirable that the following words may be added at the end of section 21(2)(c) :

"or for arriving at the truth in respect of the facts alleged by one party and denied by the other"

Section 11 provides that in every suit or proceeding to which the Family Court applies, the proceedings—

(a) may be held in camera, if the Family Court so desires; and

(b) shall be so held, if either party so desires.

Professional Assistance to the Family Court

A theme that recurs throughout the Family Courts Act is that of professional assistance, that is to say, the assistance of experts to the Family Court. The provisions in this regard are scattered throughout the Act and the experts envisaged by the Act may be of the following categories :

(i) Persons engaged in social welfare.
(ii) Counsellors.
(iii) Medical experts.
(iv) Persons engaged in promoting the welfare of the family.
(v) Legal experts.
(vi) Any other person whose association with a Family Court would enable it to exercise its jurisdiction more effectively in accordance with the purpose of the Act.

Assistance of Medical Experts and Welfare Experts

Section 12 of the Family Courts Act combines a number of propositions, crowded together at one place. It will be convenient to analyse the section, so as to bring out its salient features. The persons whose services can be secured by the Family Courts under section 12 fall in two types, namely—

(i) medical experts; and
(ii) certain persons (described in the marginal note to the section as "welfare experts").

So far as medical experts are concerned, there is no elaboration in the section, except that their services may be secured for the purpose of assisting the Court in discharging the functions imposed on it by the Act.

So far as welfare experts are concerned, the wording of the provision combines within itself certain refinements. The complex structure of the section tends to obscure these refinements of detail and it may, therefore, be convenient to re-state the gist of this part of the section as under :

(i) The Family Court may secure the services of such persons for the purpose of assisting the Court in discharging the functions imposed by the Act.
(ii) The person must preferably be a woman, where available.
(iii) Such persons may or may not be related to the parties.
(iv) This category includes a person "professionally engaged in promoting the welfare of the family".

However, it should be pointed out that it is contemplated by the Act that they may not necessarily be professional welfare experts. The marginal note to section 12, in so far as it contains the expression "welfare experts", if taken literally, is likely to give a wrong impression. The position will be clear if one reproduces the material part of section 12 (omitting ingredients which are not important for the point at present under discussion). So reproduced, the section would read as under :

> "12. In every suit or proceeding, it shall be open to a Family Court to secure the services of . . . such persons as the Court may think fit, for the purposes of assisting the Family Court in discharging the functions imposed by this Act."

It will be seen that the mention of welfare experts, as found in the section, is only in inclusive portion (deliberately not quoted in the above reproduction). It does not exhaust the categories of persons whose assistance can be taken by the Family Court (by virtue of the terms of the section as reproduced above). The only limitation is, that the securing of their services must be for the purpose of assisting the Family Court in discharging its statutory functions.

It is also necessary to say a few words about the "medical experts" envisaged by section 12. Here again, the limitation is that their services can be secured for the purpose of assisting the Family Court in discharging its functions. Beyond this, the section does not give any indication of the categories of persons whose services are permitted to be utilised by the Family Court. The functions exercisable by the Family Court are integrally linked with its jurisdiction. This jurisdiction extends to the suits and proceedings enumerated in section 7(1), Explanation. It follows that—

(a) if a question arises before the Family Court in any suit or proceeding of the nature mentioned in section 7(1), Explanation, and

(b) for the determination of that question, the Family Court needs the services of a medical expert, then his services could be secured. Rules made under the Act can regulate the procedure to be resorted to, for securing such services and the remuneration to be paid to the medical expert. But in other respects the section leaves the matter elastic. And it would appear, that on any question that arises before the Family Court in a suit or proceeding which is properly within its competence, it can secure the services, *inter alia*, of a medical expert under section 12.

Precise category of medical experts to be consulted, will naturally depend on the range, quality and dimensions of the questions at issue in the particular proceeding. For example, if the proceeding is for getting a declaration of nullity of marriage [section 7(1), Explanation (a)] and the question at issue relates to the alleged impotence of a spouse, then the service of a gynaecologist can be secured by the Family Court. Again, if the legitimacy of a child is at issue [section 7(1), Explanation (e)], then an expert in genetics can be consulted.

The question may be raised as to whether a provision like section 12 is needed at all and as to what its precise significance is. The answer lies in the opening of the sanction. "It *shall* be open to a Family Court to secure the services. . . ."

The section, in a sense, *expands* the power of the Family Court (in contrast with an ordinary civil court), and places at its disposal an additional mechanism for the better discharge of its functions. In the absence of such an express provision, it could have been argued that the Family Court (like any other civil court) is required to follow the ordinary procedure, under which the Court has to depend almost exclusively on the material produced by the parties, and cannot explore avenues of its own, for finding the facts. The section eliminates the possibility of any such argument being raised.

While permitting the Family Court to secure the services of (i) medical reports and (ii) "such persons . . . as it thinks fit," the section does not, in so many words, lay down the uses to which this power can be put. But some guidance in this regard is provided by the words "for the purposes of assisting in Family Court in discharging the *functions* imposed by this Act." Now, the basic *function* to be performed by a Family Court is that of exercising the jurisdiction otherwise exercisable by the courts mentioned in section 7(1), main paragraph, in respect of the proceedings enumerated in section 7(1), Explanation.

In brief, the Family Courts are expected to promote conciliation in, and to secure speedy settlement of, disputes relating to marriage and family affairs, as has been put in the long title of the Act. Now, the Family Court (like any other court) would normally deal with questions of :

(i) fact;
(ii) law; and
(iii) discretion.

Theoretically, the enabling power conferred by section 12 can be employed to deal with each of the three types of questions mentioned above. However, the power conferred by the section is eminently suited to deal with questions of fact and (to some extent) questions of judicial discretion. So far as questions of laws are concerned, there is a more specific provision in section 13 of the Act. As regards questions of fact, some illustrations have been already offered; and many more can be thought of. But it is in the realm of questions of discretion, that such devices would become useful.

Discretionary Powers in the Judicial Process

The discretionary powers that arise in the judicial process are represented by the vast residual jurisdiction that comes to reside with judge, when, after arriving at findings of fact and formulating conclusions of law, the judge must still come to a decision about the relief to be awarded. The discretion regarding relief is there, because the judge may have to choose between two or more options. For example, if the question is of awarding custody of the children of a marriage which is going to be, or has been dissolved by the Family Court, then the judge has to choose the party to whom the custody should be awarded. He has also to deal with the connected question of allowing access (to the child) to the "non-custodial parent". Incidentally, custody and access are both of equal importance in matrimonial proceedings. Ordinarily, while granting custody to one parent, the judge should consider also the question of allowing access to the other parent, so that the child may not be deprived of the physical company and emotional support of either parent. In deciding such questions, the judge is not concerned merely with findings of fact or with conclusions of law.

No doubt, facts as found and the law as applicable, have to be borne in mind, because it is in their light that the judge has to approach the question of the precise order to be passed. But, since so many alternatives are available to the judge when passing the orders regarding custody and access, the element of discretion residing with the judge is undeniable. Now, in deciding such delicate issues in a matrimonial proceeding, the judge may welcome the assistance of persons who would be able to assist him in the discharge of this important discretionary function. The persons whom the judge may consult for this purpose may be relatives of the parties, but they need not be so. This is made clear by section 12, Family Courts Act. They may be persons professionally engaged in the welfare of the family, but, again, the choice is not confined to them. There are other avenues open for exploration. For example, the judge may utilise the services of a teacher with whom the child is intimate, or a classmate of the child of appropriate age. A competent psychiatrist would also be useful, provided the psychiatrist is able to spend some time with the child.

For the sake of convenience, facts, law and discretion have been dealt with separately in the above sub-paragraphs. But this is not intended to imply that in actual practice, there is such a rigid fragmentation or compartmentalisation or formal chronological division. In actual practice, facts, law and discretion intermingle with each other, at more stages than one. Moreover, the broad objective of the Family Courts Act is to promote conciliation in, and secure speedy settlement of, disputes within its jurisdiction. This is well put in the long title of the Act and is reinforced by section 12. There are no other limitations, boundaries or fetters on the power conferred on the Court by section

12. Thus, the range of discretion conferred by the section itself is very vast, in point of substance.

If, as stated above, the power conferred by section 12 is very vast in point of substance, one has next to examine whether there are any procedural restrictions in this regard. From the language of section 12, there appear to be none. Subject to the rules to be made under sections 21 and 23 of the Act, the procedure to be adopted by the Family Court while resorting to section 12 is left undefined. This seems to be a deliberate decision of the legislature and is in harmony with the approach of the legislature in dealing with procedure generally. Thus, while sub-sections (1) and (2) of section 10 make certain provisions as to matters of procedure, that section itself ends with sub-section (3) quoted below :

> "(3) Nothing in sub-section (1) or sub-section (2) shall prevent a Family Court from laying down *its own procedure* with a view to arrive at a settlement in respect of the subject matter of the suit or proceedings or at the truth of the facts alleged by one party and denied by the other".

So long as the twin goals mentioned in section 10(3) are kept in mind, namely—

(i) arriving at a settlement, and
(ii) arriving at the truth about facts in issue,

the Family Court can follow its own procedure—subject of course to the principles of natural justice.

This unfettered procedural freedom, allowed to the Family Court by section 10(3) in express terms, is also the implicit postulate underlying section 12 which (by its silence on the subject) leaves to the Family Court a similarly unrestricted choice in procedural matters when utilising the power conferred by section 12.

Of course, as indicated above, the principles of justice have to be followed. Hence, to take a hypothetical illustration, if a Family Court proposes to rely on the opinion of a "medical expert" whose services it has "secured" under section 12, it is expected to communicate to the parties the gist of the opinion and to allow the parties to rebut that opinion in an appropriate manner. To read such a limitation in section 12 is not to do violence to the language of the section. Rather, such a limitation flows from the very language of section 12, which describes the object of such consultation as that of assisting the Family Court in discharging the functions imposed by this Act. The dominant themes of the Act are (i) to promote conciliation and (ii) to secure speedy settlement. Each of these themes envisages the involvement of the parties in the process of litigation, not as mere contestants, but as participants in a constructive endeavour.

Natural justice is nothing but the obverse of the concept of involvement of the parties whose case is to be heard by an impartial judge. Subject to this broad limitation, section 12, Family Courts Act leaves ample procedural freedom to the judge presiding over a Family Court, when utilising the services of the persons mentioned in section 12(c).

What about the procedure to be followed by those persons themselves? Here again, the Act does not lay down any specific requirements, except (i) those flowing from the very object underlying the utilisation of their services or (ii) those specifically imposed by the rules. Of course, the person whose services are secured, if he is a professional, will ordinarily follow the procedure to which his own professional discipline has acclimatised him; and this will automatically have the effect of bringing in a certain element of method, system and order in his own proceedings.

Right to Legal Representation

In contrast with the liberal and open approach shown by section 12, section 13, Family Courts Act adopts a negative stance, by providing that no party shall be entitled to be represented by a legal practitioner before the Family Court. This prohibition, as contained in the main paragraph of the section, is sought to be fortified by the equally strong words: "Notwithstanding anything contained in any law." There is one more *non obstante* provision in section 20, which gives an overriding effect *to every provision* of the Act.

To some extent, the rigour of section 13, main paragraph is mitigated by the proviso to section 13, under which, if the Family Court considers it necessary in the interests of justice, it may seek the assistance of a legal expert as *amicus curiae*. Where the court seeks such assistance, the fees to be paid to the legal expert are to be regulated by rules to be made by the State Government under section 23(2)(d). The person to be consulted has to be "legal expert".

This expression is much wider than a legal practitioner. The person may, for example, be a retired judge, a legal academician, a civil servant or a private person with knowledge of the law or a legal author. Of course, his opinion is not binding on the Court. The use of the term "*amicus curiae*" (friend of the court), indicates that such a person will not put forth the case of this or that party. Rather, he will assist the Court in arriving at a proper conclusion on issues of law. The key words in section 13, proviso are : "If the Family Court considers it *necessary* in the interest of justice". Thus, the twin requirements to be borne in mind by the Court seeking such assistance are—

(i) necessity, and
(ii) interest of justice.

Of course, under an earlier provision of the Act, rules made by the State Government in consultation with the High Court may provide, *inter alia*, for the association, with a Family Court, of any other person whose association, with a Family Court would enable it to exercise its jurisdiction more effectively in accordance with the purposes of this Act. This provision is undoubtedly wide enough to permit legal as well as non-legal experts (including even intelligent and knowledgeable law students), to be associated with Family Courts in accordance with the rules, "if the association would enable the Family Court to exercise its jurisdiction more effectively in accordance with the purposes of the Act." The purposes of the Act have been already dwelt upon in early paragraphs. One of them is speedy settlement of disputes concerning marriage and family affairs. Such speedy settlement may, on a given occasion, render it desirable that independent legal advice of high quality may be made available to the Family Court. It should be remembered that in the scheme of the Family Courts Act, persons without legal qualification can be appointed to the Family Court. Presiding Officers so recruited may, on occasions desire to consult a legal expert, and section 13, proviso, will be very useful for them. Of course, it is desirable that they should be given some legal orientation. This is, in fact, contemplated by the Act. Section 4(3)(c) (applicable to such persons) envisages that the Central Government, with the concurrence of the Chief Justice of India, may prescribe the qualification to be satisfied by them.

However, there still arises the wider question. Is the prohibition against legal representation, incorporated in section 13 main paragraph, justified? In this writer's view, it is not. And this writer's view is, that section 13 should be revised as under :

> "13. *Legal representation.* (1) A party to a suit or proceeding before a Family Court shall be entitled as of right to be represented by a legal practitioner of his choice.
>
> (2) The Family Court may permit a person other than a legal practitioner to represent a party in the interests of justice.
>
> (3) If the Family Court considers it necessary in the interests of justice, it may seek the assistance of a legal expert as *amicus curiae* or as an advocate of a child whose interest may be affected".

Evidence

Apart from provisions relating to procedure proper, the Family Courts Act contains certain special sections relating to evidence. These sections have the effect of (a) relaxing the general laws of evidence as contained in the Indian Evidence Act, 1872, so as to enlarge the sphere of "relevant facts and admissible evidence" (as envisaged in the Evidence Act) by an enabling provision applicable to Family Courts (section 14); (b) simplifying the procedure for recording the evidence of witnesses, so as to modify the procedure envisaged in this regard in the Code of Civil Procedure, 1908 as applicable to Family Courts (section 15); and (c) permitting the giving of evidence on affidavits, so as to *supplement* the provisions of the Code of Civil Procedure, 1908, as applicable to Family (section 16).

Special provisions falling in categories (b) and (c) mentioned above, made by sections 15 and 16 of the Family Courts Act, apply also in relation to proceedings for maintenance under section 125, Code of Criminal Procedure, 1973, where such proceedings are heard by Family Courts.

Reception of Evidence by Family Courts under Section 14

The most important provision on the subject of evidence is that contained in section 14 of the Family Courts Act, which reads as under :

> "14. *Application of Indian Evidence Act, 1872.* A Family Court may receive as evidence, any report, statement, document, information or matter that may, in its opinion, assist it to deal effectively with a dispute, whether or not the same would be otherwise relevant or admissible under the Indian Evidence Act, 1872".

The very wide sweep and drastic nature of this provision will be better understood, if it is broken up and projected as under :

(1) A Family Court may receive as evidence –

(a) any report;

(b) any statement;

(c) any document;

(d) any information; or

(e) any matter, that may, in its opinion, assist it to deal effectively with a dispute.

(2) The above proposition applies, whether or not the report etc. would be otherwise relevant or admissible under the Indian Evidence Act, 1872.

The permission to receive any report, statement etc. undeniably permits hearsay evidence to be given, particularly because of the overriding liberty given by the words "whether or not the same would be otherwise relevant *or admissible*" etc. This, in effect, overrides section 60 of the Evidence Act, and expands the scope of section 32 of the same Act (in their application to Family Courts).

The permission to receive as evidence any documents, information or matter seems to indefinitely expand the area of relevant facts, as envisaged in the Evidence Act, particularly because of the words "whether or not the same would be *relevant* or admissible under the Indian Evidence Act, 1872" which occur towards the end of section 14, Family Courts Act. This, if effect, enlarges the scope of sections 5-55, Evidence Act (the group of sections mainly dealing with the relevance of facts). To put it more strongly, section 14, Family Courts Act, practically abolishes the distinction between "logical" relevancy and "legal" relevancy, as discussed by text book writers on evidence. In fact, one can go a bit further and say, that section 14, Family Courts Act, even goes beyond the strict concept of logical relevance in the objective sense. By permitting the Family Court to receive as evidence "any report, statement, document, information or matter that may, *in its opinion*, assist it to deal effectively with a dispute", section 14 enacts a *substantive* test, based on the court's opinion, rather than an *objective* test based on the inherent probative force of one fact as proving another fact. One example will make it clear. If, in a proceeding for divorce, the question is, whether a wife who is a party to the proceeding before the Family Court, is telling the truth and there are reports (or there is information) that she is a person of generally immoral character, the Family Court can receive as evidence those reports etc. if the report etc. would, in the opinion of the Court, enable it to deal effectively with a dispute. Sections 51-55, Evidence Act, which exclude evidence of bad character (subject to specified exceptions), would not come in the way, because of the last 17 words of section 14, Family Courts Act: "whether or not the same would be otherwise relevant or "admissible under the Indian Evidence Act, 1872".

Whether this consequence was intended or not, is a matter for discussion; and it may be suggested that the point needs serious legislative attention. However, on the present wording of section, the interpretation submitted above seems to be almost inescapable.

Take another example. A husband sues his wife for divorce on the ground that the wife has committed adultery with an office colleague of hers. It is found that in the wife's office, disciplinary action had been taken against the wife on the basis of this very act of misbehaviour. The disciplinary order would become admissible in the divorce action if, in the opinion of the judge, this "information or matter" would assist him in effectively dealing with the dispute. This is departure from the position prevailing in the Evidence Act. The disciplinary order would be (technically) hearsay and would be excluded by section 60, Evidence Act. It does not appear to be admissible under sections 40-44, Evidence Act, dealing with judgements in earlier proceedings.

Criticism of Section 14

What the legislature probably intended by section 14 was, that where and in so far as the Presiding Officer of a Family Court is endeavouring to promote a consensual settlement between the parties, the judge *at that stage* should not be hidebound by the Evidence Act. But it needs to be pointed out that when efforts are going on towards a compromise, Evidence Act has hardly any role to play. At that stage, no evidence is recorded. In fact, no trial is held. No judgement is given. Rather, the parties come to an agreed solution. The judge is not going to decide any issue and for that particular stage no special provision of the nature enacted in section 14, Family Courts Act, is needed.

If no compromise is effected and the trial has to be held on the merits of the case, then, to make each and every report, statement, document, information or matter receivable in evidence before a Family Court, totally disregarding the Evidence Act, would lead to drastic consequences, as already elaborated. It would make all kinds of hearsay and gossip admissible. It would bring in evidence of bad character. It would indefinitely and unpredictably enlarge the scope of the facts that can be brought on the record. There hardly appears to a justification for such a drastic approach. The law needs amendment.

In this writer's very humble submission, section 14 of the Family Courts Act should be deleted. It may be argued that section 14 is not so drastic as is assumed above, because the Court will let in evidence under this section only if, *in its opinion*, the report etc. would assist the court in dealing effectively with the dispute. However, this argument misses the point, that a provision leaving the matters to the *subjective* decision of the presiding judge is bound to open up an immensely vast zone of differing approaches from judge to judge. It will thereby lead to undue discrimination, even if it be an honest variation from case to case. It is true that even under the Evidence Act, evaluation of evidence can vary from judge to judge. But, if one gives a blank cheque to the judge as regards the *basic data* that is to constitute the foundation of fact finding, then the result would be that each judge would, in effect, be creating a law of evidence of his own—and that too, a separate law of evidence for each proceeding that may come up before the judge. This cannot be a satisfactory approach.

It is further to be pointed out, that in matrimonial cases (as in ordinary civil litigation), the fact finding process is a very essential part of the total exercise, if there is to be a trial on the merits. Once the efforts at conciliation fail, and the possibilities of a settlement recede into the background, the stage is naturally set for a contest between the parties. Unfortunate though a contest on the facts may be, and however acrimonious it may be, if it has to be fought, let it be fought according to well tested methods. In the absence of compelling reasons, such matters ought not to be brought within the range of absolute and unguided discretion. There is always a possibility, that even if the judge has exercised his discretion honestly, one party will still be aggrieved and then the acrimony will be accentuated, instead of being mitigated.

Applicability of Evidence Act to Family Courts : A Point of Drafting

So far, only matters of substance concerning section 14 have been discussed. There remains to be considered a point of drafting, arising out of this section. Section 14 carries the marginal note "Applicability of Indian Evidence Act, 1872." But, curiously, there is no direct provision in the section to the effect either that the Evidence Act is applicable to Family Courts or that it is not applicable to Family Courts. Of course, the better view seems to be, that the section assumes that the Evidence Act will apply, but at the same time, gives an overriding power to the judge of the Family Court to receive irrelevant or inadmissible report etc., if he is of the opinion that such a course would assist him in effectively disposing of the dispute. If one takes the view that the Evidence Act does not apply, then some curious results would follow. For example, several provisions of the Act as to (i) the competence of witnesses, (ii) the privilege in the law of evidence, (iii) order of examination of witnesses, (iv) questions that can or cannot be asked in examination-in-chief and cross-examination, (v) procedure for contradicting a witness, (iv) procedure for refreshing the memory of a witness, and (vii) judge's power to put questions etc. to a witness, would become inapplicable. That could hardly be the intention of the law-makers. Just as, in regard to procedure, section 10(1) of the Family Courts Act expressly provides that, subject to the other provisions of the Act and the rules, the Code of Civil Procedure, 1908 will apply to a Family Court and that Court will be deemed to be a civil court, similarly, the Act *intends* that even as regards evidence, subject to the provisions of sections 14 to 16 and the rules made under the Family Courts Act, the Evidence Act will apply to a Family Court and it will be deemed to be a civil court for that purpose. This proposition is not expressed in the Act, but that seems to be the implied assumption. In the author's submission, this should be made clear by inserting a suitable provision at an appropriate place in the Family Courts Act. If section 14 (as it stands at present) is deleted, such a provision can be inserted in its place, as (substituted) section 14.

Evidentiary Privilege in Family Courts

There still remains to be considered the question of evidentiary privilege in proceedings before Family Courts. As submitted above, those provisions of the Evidence Act which are not expressly overridden by section 14, Family Courts Act, should be regarded as applicable to Family Courts, notwithstanding the somewhat incomplete drafting of section 14. These provisions include, *inter alia*, provisions relating to privileges of parties and witnesses (except where the Evidence Act itself takes away the privilege in regard to matrimonial proceedings). On any other view, there would arise very serious consequences. For example, matters communicated between a spouse and his or her legal adviser (section 125-129, Evidence Act) would lose their protection before Family Courts. The same would apply to State secrets (even though their scope is now much narrowed down). This would not be satisfactory.

While on the topic of privilege, it would be proper to mention that under the Evidence Act, communications made "without prejudice" are protected from disclosure. These communications are made by one party to another to promote a settlement of the litigation. It is obvious that in regard to proceedings before Family Courts, this particular privilege possesses great utility and has to be preserved.

IRRETRIEVABLE BREAKDOWN OF MARRIAGE AS A GROUND FOR DIVORCE

GATEWAY TO LIBERATION OR OPPRESSION ?

*B. Sivaramayya**

The Law Commission of India in the year 1988 invited the views of the public on introducing irretrievable breakdown as a ground for divorce under the Hindu Marriage Act, 1955 (HMA). The views on this appear to be sharply divided. Seemingly the educated urban women prefer the ground. However, one must be sure that a vocal minority does not jeopardize the interests of a silent majority especially the under-privileged and rural women.

Background

In view of the colonial heritage, trends in English law influence our law strongly on some aspects. Originally divorce under the matrimonial law of England was based on fault grounds like adultery, desertion, cruelty etc. But during the sixties there was a significant change in thinking on this aspect. It was asserted that marital fault is symptom of breakdown of marriage and not the cause of breakdown. A group appointed by Archbishop of Canterbury in their report *Putting Asunder* was in favour of divorce based on breakdown of marriage. *Putting Asunder* was considered by the Law Commission in England in their report *Reform of the Ground of Divorce : the Field of Choice*. Based on a consideration of the *Field of Choice* and differing from it in some material respects, the Matrimonial Causes Act, 1973 recognised irretrievable breakdown of marriage as the only ground for divorce. Respondent's adultery, desertion and conduct (cruelty) which would have operated as grounds for divorce under the

*Former Professor, Law Faculty, Delhi University

prior law are regarded as facts which give rise to a presumption of breakdown of marriage.

Originally under the Hindu Marriage Act, 1955 divorce was based on the fault principle. Subsequently non-fault grounds found place under Section 13 I-A. They are : (1) Where a decree for judicial separation has been passed and the parties have not resumed co-habitation for a period of one year or more, and (2) where a decree for restitution of conjugal rights has been passed and there has been no restitution of conjugal rights for a period of one year or more. In the above cases either party is entitled to ask for divorce. Divorce by mutual consent was introduced in 1976. The Law Commission in the 71st Report recommended the introduction of irretrievable breakdown of marriage as a ground for divorce. The report was given by the Commission consisting of two members only, the Chairman and Member-Secretary. The latter being in the position of a bureaucrat cannot be expected to dissent from the Chairman. The Ministry of Education, Department of Social Welfare expressed the view that the ground was redundant in view of the already existing grounds for divorce.

The Law Commission's proposals differed from the English Law in three respects :

1. Under the English Law irretrievable breakdown constitutes the sole ground for divorce; whereas under the Indian Law it is an additional ground to the ones already existing. This accords with the view expressed by the Law Commission in England.

2. Under English Law if the parties are living separately for a period of 5 years without consent it will be considered as evidence of breakdown of marriage whereas under the proposed law the period is reduced to 3 years on the ground that in India, it takes a long time to get relief in matrimonial cases. The questionnaire issued in 1988 among other things wanted to elicit whether the period should be increased to five years.

3. In English Law the court is entitled to refuse relief on the grounds of financial or other hardship; but under the recommendations of the Law Commission the court is entitled to refuse relief on the ground of grave financial hardship only.

When a bill was introduced in Parliament in 1982 the women's organisations voiced their opposition to the Bill on the ground that many women in rural areas live apart from their husbands as they (husbands) go to cities for earning their livelihood; that unscrupulous husbands would be in a position to take advantage of such separation and get divorce. They pointed out that unless financial security of women after divorce is assured by means of a provision for a share in the assets acquired by the husband during the subsistence of the marriage, irretrievable breakdown of marriage would be inimical to the interests of women. Conceding the validity of the objections, the Bill was allowed to lapse. It is pertinent to point out in this context the position taken by the Committee on the Status of Women. That Committee while it recommended the ground, but considered it as one among the package along with the other more important proposal *viz.* on divorce, a woman should be entitled to a share (at least 1/3 in the property of the husband).

It should be pointed out that the questionnaire of the Law Commission issued in 1988 proceeds on the (simplistic) assumption that Family Courts are functioning and therefore the introduction of the proposed ground for divorce is justified. In this context it is relevant to recall the statement of Prof. Jaffer Hussain made on the basis of the U.S. and English experience, as to the follow-up measures needed while introducing the irretrievable breakdown as a ground for divorce.[1]

> There have been two reform movements in the area of divorce in United States and England. First, the recognition of breakdown of marriage as a basis for dissolution, secondly the establishment of Family Courts and the provision for reconciliation services, when we import the concept of breakdown from the Anglo-American Law, we must also make suitable alternative arrangements in procedural law. Suggesting changes in the substantive law without a corresponding change would be like enacting Hamlet without the Prince of Denmark. As stated by Llewellyn "technique without ideals is a menace . . . ideals without technique are amass.

It should be pointed that the assumption of the Law Commission that the establishment of Family Courts justifies the introduction of the ground is questionable. Only a beginning has been made in this direction. For example, there is no Family Court in the Metropolitan City of Delhi owing to the opposition of lawyers. In the States where they have been introduced they are woefully short of actual needs and grossly understaffed with respect to para legal services.

At a seminar organised on January 28, 1989 on the question, some academics had occasion to state their views on the subject. A reference will be made to these now. Prof. Susheela Kaushik asked : Is it too much to say that the safeguards would be available for urban and rural women in the near future? The safeguards which were not existing in 1982 are they in force now? (It may be recalled that similar fears were voiced by Dr. Vina Mazumdar and Prof. Lotika Sarkar who were members of the Committee on the Status of Women).

Prof. A.M. Shah, Department of Sociology, Delhi University, pointed out that divorce as well as remarriage were common among the lower castes; that since upper castes form a very small proportion of the total population of Hindus, the divorce law under the HMA applies to a very small section of the society and that in this section the view that marriage is indissoluble still persists. He stated that a certain sub-section of this section, *viz.;* urbanized and Westernized section or modernized section was demanding liberalization of the divorce law and the proposed amendment would help this tiny section only.

It is to be noted that even in groups where customary divorce prevails, increasingly resort is made to the State Legal System, that is, the HMA owing to urbanization and other factors. Again it is a moot point whether women are free agents in choosing their partners. If they have financial security, they are likely to be free in stating their choices.

Giving his views on this question Prof. Upendra Baxi observed : first, only women should be allowed to take advantage of this new ground; second, that a means-test should be adopted for granting the ground, that is, the ground should be available where the women is in a position to maintain her children, say, to those having property of 10 lakhs; and third, the possible impact of the provision on the dowry market should be studied; namely would it lead, to an extension of the dowry market or a restraint on it?

The first point has much to commend in it. The analogy of option of puberty which is available to a woman only under the amendments to the HMA in 1976 is apposite. As regards the second; it is not clear whether in his view both the conditions should be cumulative or alternative proposals. But either way it is open to a serious objection, *viz.* will it be constitutionally valid? Means test is unexceptionable in giving advantage to the underprivileged for facilities like legal aid or giving scholarships. But can it be used to give an advantage to the rich? The suggestion is evading the basic question of policy whether the ground is desirable. If the answer is yes, there is no reason why it should be denied in case of a woman, who does not have means. Thus we are back to square one, namely, unless backed-up by property rights and economic security the ground should not be introduced. Otherwise a woman seeking the ground under the pressure or false impression or by cajoling will not be protected.

The third suggestion, attractive as it may appear to be, involves a difficulty. Should the ground be introduced first and its effects studied later? Obviously one cannot study the impact without introducing the ground. If so, it renders the potential victim a kind of object for experimentation. Again what if in a vast country like India the findings differ?

It is indeed surprising that the Law Commission is trying to revive recommendations in the 71st Report in the absence of any attempt to buttress the financial position of a divorced woman, especially with respect to existing provisions relating to maintenance or by a provision for a share in acquisition of the property of the husband which provide for the financial security. For example, under the existing law of Hindus on divorce the only right of a divorced woman is to get maintenance. If for example, a divorce takes place after 20 years of marriage does maintenance confer on her financial security? Maintenance is not sufficient to get her even accommodation suitable for her needs in many cases. On the death of the husband even this meagre right is lost. Further, even after a wife or a divorced wife secures a decree, after some years the husband or the former husband contumaciously stops payment of the amount and the woman is forced to approach the court once again. It may be recalled that 73rd Report of the Law Commission recommended that erring husbands, who contumaciously stop payment of maintenance to their wives, should be punished with 6 months rigorous imprisonment. This Report has not been implemented as yet. Why these reports are allowed to gather dust? The proposal made by the Committee on the Status of Women that a woman on divorce should be entitled to a share in the assets of her husband is yet to be considered seriously either by the Law Commission or by the Government. The clause relating to "grave financial hardship" will hardly save innocent wives unwilling for divorce from the uncertainties of interpretation and perils of litigation. Under these circumstances, will the ground be a gateway for liberation or of oppression to married women?

NOTES AND REFERENCES

1. S. Jaffer Hussain, *Marriage Breakdown and Divorce Law Reform in Contemporary Society* 218 (1983).

EDITOR'S NOTE

The enactment of Section 13(1-a) in the Hindu Marriage Act, 1955 and section 27(2) (i) and (ii) in the Special Marriage Act, 1954, by way of amendments is indicative of a deliberate beginning, though in a limited way towards introduction of breakdown of marriage as a ground for divorce.[1]

A further step towards the recognition of this principle was taken in 1976 when divorce by mutual consent was inserted into the Hindu Marriage Act. (The special Marriage Act, already had this ground.) This however, is also not a very satisfactory provision as it does not work where, despite an utterly wrecked marriage, one of them does not want a divorce. The result is that the parties are neither divorced nor living together. They are impelled to live together only *in Law*. Sometimes both the parties may not be at fault and yet the marriage may not work. Nonetheless, the law cannot provide a meaningful relief because of the absence of a 'ground'. Our courts have often found themselves tied down by the technicality of law and refused relief where it ought to have been given had the law recognised breakdown of marriage as a ground for divorce. In *Ramkali* v. *Gopal Das*[2] it was observed:

> "It would not be a practical and realistic approach, indeed it would be unreasonable and inhuman, to compel the parties to keep up the facade of marriage even though the rift between them is complete and there are no prospects of their ever living together as husband and wife."

Justice Rajindar Sachar in, *Gulab Rai Sharma* v. *Pushpa Devi*[3] lamented the 'technicalities of Law' which made him helpless in giving relief to the appellant husband. The marriage had a chequered history and was practically broken. The court, however, could not label the conduct of the respondent wife as a 'fault' so as to entitle the husband for relief. The husband was not at fault either but, as remarked by the court:

> "An unfortunate situation has arisen where none of the parties are at fault, but still they do not have the grace and sensitivity to agree to a divorce by mutual consent. . . . Law at present is quite rigid and the human

sensitivity which should have found some way either to smoothen the relations between the parties or to put an end to it has not triumphed."[4]

With a heavy heart, Justice Sachar was left with no choice except to dismiss the husband's appeal.

It is submitted that in the absence of such ground, a party who is bent upon seeking relief will adopt dubious methods, cook up allegations, purchase witnesses and what not, only to fit into the requisite clause or ground which can enable it to get relief. This not only creates more bitterness between the parties and children but also makes a mockery of the law and court.

A forcibly maintained relationship and unavailability of divorce is also bound to give rise to other unhappy situations like adultery, extra-marital relationships, delinquency amongst children and other forms of social maladjustments.

With proper provisions safeguarding the interest of women and children, it is time that introducing irretrievable breakdown of marriage as a ground for divorce be given serious thought.

As observed by one scholar:

> "(A) dead marriage is no less dead because only one [or even none] of the parties is demonstrably at fault. It must be observed. . . that demonstrable fault is frequently the result of, rather than the cause of, marital breakdown. . . . It is the public interest in private morality, in marriage as an institution, that is best served by terminating marriages that have failed. The outmoded policy of suspending in limbo the offending spouse is the wrong remedy in so far as public morality is concerned."[5]

It is in the interest of all parties that a practically dead marriage be given a legally decent burial so that whatever remains of the relationship could be salvaged.

NOTES AND REFERENCES

1. See Kusum "Irretrievable Breakdown of Marriage—A Ground for Divorce" *1978 JILI 288-303*.
2. ILR (1971) Delhi 6(F.B.).
3. ILR (1979) II Delhi 220.
4. *Id.* at 226.
5. Michael J. Whaling "The No Fault Concept : Is this the Final Stage in the Evolution of Divorce" *47 Notre Dame Lawyer* 966-67(1971-72).

MARRIED WOMEN'S DOMICILE—A LEGAL FRAMEWORK

*Lakshmi Jambholkar**

The term 'domiclile' means a dwelling place, abode or one's legally recognised place of residence.[1] Domicile, in the legal sense,[2] denotes 'permanent home'. Functionally, domicile indicates the personal law that governs the questions relating to status.

Not long ago, married woman was universally regarded as totally a dependent person on her husband. This probably led to the idea that husband and wife constitute one person. In law, generally, as a dependent person, a married woman was incapable of having a domicile of her own. After marriage the husband's domicile was transmitted to the wife, continuing during the subsistence of marriage and also changing along with the husband's domicile. The rule of unity of matrimonial domicile for purposes of Court's jurisdiction in matters of matrimonial remedies thus came into being. At common law a married woman had a domicile dependent on that of her husband irrespective of whether they are separated either informally or on the basis of decree of judicial separation.[3] The rule had had the effect of suspending the legal existence of the woman during the subsistence of marriage. English law amply demonstrates the sufferings of a married woman as a result of the theory of common domicile for husband and wife. In England, this rule of common domicile combined with the rule that a married woman cannot acquire a domicile separate from her husband produced serious hardships and injustice particularly in case of the deserted wives of overseas employed (English) personnel. The English wife's troubles became compounded when the divorce jurisdiction was based by English Courts solely on husband's domicile.

*Reader, Law Faculty, Delhi University, Delhi

After a period of hesitation the Privy Council finally ruled in *Le Mesurier* v. *Le Mesurier*[4] that the English Courts have jurisdiction to dissolve a marriage only if the spouses are domiciled in England at the time of the commencement of the proceedings and that the domicile of the wife means that of the husband in the true and full sense of the term at that time.

No other factor was considered relevant. Consequently the wife found herself in most difficult situation. She could not petition to the Court even in cases where she was exploited at the hands of a husband who not only left the shores of England but had altogether forgotten his English wife's existence. The rule that in no circumstances can a married woman have a domicile different from that of husband attracted juristic criticism.[5] Indeed this stand contradicts all modern ideas of sex equality.

In order to help the wife out of such hard situations it was held in later cases[6] that the wife possessed a domicile in England, sufficient to enable her to obtain divorce although such a rule amounted to giving up the rule that the wife's domicile is that of her husband whatever or wherever that may be. Judicial precedents have thus been instrumental in improving the wife's situation. The redoubtable Lord Denning condemned the rule of husband's domicile as a basis for matrimonial jurisdiction in *Gray* v. *Formosa*[7] as the "last barbaric relic of a wife's servitude".[8]

Besides judicial contribution, some relief was provided by legislation. The first statutory exception to the rule of husband's domicile was introduced by the Matrimonial Causes Act,1937 (by sec.13). It provided that the Court shall have jurisdiction to entertain proceedings by a wife, notwithstanding that the husband is not domiciled in England : if (i) the wife has been deserted by the husband or (ii) the husband has been deported from the United Kingdom under any law for the time being in force relating to deportation, and the husband was immediately before the desertion or deportation domiciled in England.

The inadequacy of these provisions is that they applied only to cases of husband's deportation or cases where he has been guilty of desertion provided also he was domiciled in England immediately before such deportation or desertion. Parliament therefore introduced another exception to the rule of domicile in the Matrimonial Causes Act, 1950, Sec. 18(1) (b) which was later re-enacted in the Matrimonial Causes Act,1965 as Sec. 40(1) (b), which provided:

The Court shall have jurisdiction to the proceedings by a wife, notwithstanding that the husband is not domiciled in England, if (i) the wife is resident in England and has been ordinarily resident there for a period of 3 years immediately preceding and (ii) the husband is not domiciled in any other part of the U.K. or in the Channel Islands or the Isle of Man.

This was indeed a positive step in the direction of freeing a harassed wife from the holds of the rigid rule of husband's domicile. Even so, it had shortcomings in many respects. These rules made the wife wait for a long period of 3 years prior to the institution of the proceedings and in addition retained domicile in England as a connecting factor in its technical and strict form. The basic formulation of the concept of domicile needed re-orientation to the changing society. Thus a search for alternative connecting factors resulted in the Domicile and Matrimonial Proceedings Act, 1973 which provided two bases of jurisdiction for matrimonial causes, *viz.* domicile and habitual residence. Wife's independent domicile even after marriage is the significant contribution of this enactment. The rule of wife's domicile to be that of her husband's after marriage was thus abolished finally in 1973. According to section I of the Domicile and Matrimonial Proceedings Act, 1973, the domicile of a married woman as at any time on or after January 1st, 1974, shall, instead of being the same as her husband's by virtue of marriage, be ascertained by reference to the same factors as in the case of any other individual capable of having an independent domicile.

The doctrine of unity of domicile in the case of husband and wife is generally followed in majority of the countries as a basic rule. However, at present many countries recognise the right of a wife to have a separate domicile in statutes. Many of continental Europe and Latin American countries which follow the unity of domicile doctrine as a general rule, have recognised wife's separate domicile in the form of an exception to it. In Eastern Europe and Scandinavia including Germany, Belgium and Netherlands, there are no longer any rules curbing wives' independence in matters of domicile.[9] According to Italian Law, the wife is entitled to a separate domicile when she is judicially separated, or if her husband "is placed under guardianship" or takes up a foreign domicile (Codice Civile (1942), S. 42). Martin Wolff who opposes the wife's domicile necessarily following that of her husband's views the Swiss Code as the "soundest solution". Under the Swiss Code "the wife who is entitled to live separately may have a domicile of her own even if she has not applied for a judicial separation" (Swiss Civil Code, Art . 25, S. 2).

At present, United Kingdom, U.S.A. Canada, and many other Western countries have gone ahead and the Swiss Code had enacted legislations providing separate domicile for wife. In U.S.A., it has been viewed that "without the possibility of separate domicile for wives the American divorce system, under which wives are usually plaintiffs, would breakdown".[10]

Laws in India, which generally followed the foot prints of English Law in almost all fields, remained silent as regards the position of married woman in respect of her domicile after marriage. Since our Laws have not been amended on the lines of the English Laws of 1974, our Courts unhappily still consider married woman as a dependent person. Under the traditional notions a woman in India was never to lead an independent life on her own. "A woman is protected during her childhood by her father, during her youth by her husband and during old age by her son".[11] This thinking seemed to have paved the way for the formulation of legal conception that by valid marriage the domicile of wife invariably follows that of her husband and changes with his during coverture, on the lines of English law.

However, amongst the entire Indian Legislation in the area of personal laws only the Indian Succession Act of 1925 (part II) to a certain extent codifies principles of Private International Law relating to, domicile in India.[12] In fact it has made a bold departure albeit in the form of an exception in the case of wife's domicile from that of the English Law (that was, prior to the passing of Domicile and Matrimonial Proceedings Act,1973).[13] Thus under Section 16 a wife's domicile no longer follows that of her husband, if they are separated by the sentence of a competent court or if the husband is undergoing a sentence of transportation. It may be pointed out that though the provisions of the Indian Succession Act, 1925 (part II) have incorporated the leading principles of Private International Law pertaining to the area of domicile, strictly speaking, they have a limited application under this Act—limited in the first instance only to the cases involving succession and secondly the Act excludes its application to Hindus, Muslims, Buddhists, Sikhs or Jains.[14]

A general perusal of the situation in India of matters pertaining to married woman's domicile through various judicial pronouncements, either based on the earlier English Law or through the enforcement of the Indian Succession Act,1925, makes it very clear that during coverture a wife's domicile is that of her husband's. Indeed the statement is more than a century old in the rest of the world. The deviation that was introduced in the Indian Succession Act, by way of an exception in India has been treated as the rule in U.K. and other countries, in view of changes evidenced in the society all over the world. But the Indian Courts and the Legislative bodies are yet to be woken up to the realities.

In India, the question of married woman's domicile has also been dealt with generally besides the provisions of the Indian Succession Act,1925. The available case law on the subject amply illustrates the situation. In a pre-independence case, *Jones* v. *Jones*[15] the Lahore High Court was concerned with husband's domicile for the purposes of its divorce jurisdiction. The court proceeded in this case on a firm basic premise that the married woman's domicile is that of her husband's and that the matrimonial jurisdiction is based solely on the parties' domicile. The court clearly opined, "the important question for decision in this appeal is the domicile of the husband. The petitioner (wife) whatever may be her own domicile, has by marriage acquired the domicile of her husband."[16] In *Khambatta* v. *Khambatta*,[17] a matter concerning dissolution of marriage came up for hearing. Beaumont C.J., delivering the judgement observed that the *lex domicili* of the husband was the sole consideration on the question of the nature of marriage including the grounds of divorce irrespective of the *lex domicili* of the wife before marriage. The Calcutta High Court did not exercise jurisdiction to declare the marriage dissolved in *Noorjehan Begum* v. *Eugene Tiscenco*[18] as the parties did not have their domicile in India. In this case the petitioner, a Russian lady came to India and embraced Islam. She filed a petition for declaration under the Specific Relief Act (1 of 1887) that the marriage stood dissolved according to her personal law Islam, as her husband, a Russian who stayed back in Europe, did not accept her invitation for conversion to Islam.

The question of married woman's domicile remained unaltered in the post-independence era as well. The courts continued to rule on the same line as before. In *Rani Saeeda Khatun* v. *State of Bihar*,[19] the Patna High Court accepted the plea of a Muslim woman married to a Hindu that the husband's domicile being India she could not be asked to quit India. She also pleaded that she was incapable of acquiring a domicile in any other country during the subsistence of her marriage. This principle of unity of domicile was again upheld in *Smt. Allabandi* v. *Union of India*[20] by the Allahabad High Court where it ruled against a deportation order of a Muslim wife on the ground that her husband had an Indian domicile and that she too retained on Indian domicile. The Muslim wife was taken away to Pakistan by her parents, in this case, leaving behind her husband in India in 1947. In the wife's petition the Court applied the doctrine of unity of domicile and held her to be citizen of India under Article 5 of the Indian Constitution which confers citizenship on those who had their domicile in the territory of India at the commencement of the Constitution.[21] In *Attaullah* v. *Attaullah*[22] the Calcutta High Court did not exercise jurisdiction in a divorce petition as the petitioner's husband had domicile in Pakistan.

Indeed Rajasthan High Court in a divorce petition in *Christopher Andrew Neelakantan* v. *Mrs. Anee Neelakantan*[23] acknowledged thus; "It seems as if a married woman is under a sort of a disability in the matter of domicile . . . ." The Court confirmed that the wife's domicile follows that of her husband's and only the courts of domicile have jurisdiction for matrimonial causes.[24] In *Prakash* v. *Mst.*[25] the Jammu and Kashmir High Court had an opportunity to rule on the domicile of a widow. The case concerns with the question whether the respondent belonged to the State of Jammu and Kashmir which alone gives her capacity to hold and own immovable property in Jammu and Kashmir. The respondent claimed the status of a permanent resident of the State on the ground of her father being a State subject while she herself was a widow of a non-state subject. She was married to a person from Sialkot (now in Pakistan). The court held that since her domicile being Sialkot (that of her husband's) she cannot own immovable property in Jammu and Kashmir. In the context the court observed : ". . . the wife is incapable of acquiring a separate domicile of her own, no matter her husband may have even deserted her. Nothing short of a dissolution of marriage tie enables a married woman to acquire a separate domicile. Even on the death of her husband, a widow retains her late husband's domicile until she changes it by her own act, e.g. by re-marriage". The doctrine of unity of domicile of husband was exploited as a means to obtain admission into professional educational institution in the case of *Kakathiya Medical College* v. *Jayasri.*[26] The respondent laid her claim for admission in the medical college on the basis of her marriage to a holder of "the Mulki domicile certificate". She argued that by marriage she had acquired "Mulki domicile". Rejecting her claim the Court in this regard observed that although in law a married woman acquired the domicile of her husband after marriage, the domicile to be considered for the purpose of admission is not the legal domicile but the factum of actual residence in a particular region.[27] The court thus distinguished the purpose oriented domicile from that of the general legal domicile as understood under rules of private international law.

In matter of married woman's domicile, the Indian courts have time and again affirmed the view that wife's domicile follows that of her husband's.[28] The case law in India followed the law prevalent generally in England before 1974 when Domicile and Matrimonial Law Proceedings Act of 1973 came into force, which abolished totally wife's dependence on her husband for her domicile. Particular reference may be made to the Punjab and Haryana High Court's decision in *Teja Singh* v. *Satya,*[29] where the appellant husband who had left for higher studies in U.S.A. refuted his wife's claim for her maintenance as their marriage stood dissolved on the basis of a divorce decree secured by him from the District Court of Nevada in U.S.A. The wife's plea for her Indian domicile though her husband was living in US on the ground that she had never left the shores of India or had not visited USA at any stage of her life was rejected by the Court. The Court which squarely based its reasoning on *Le Mesurier* v. *Le Mesurier*[30] ruled that it lacked jurisdiction as it is not the court of domicile. The same case, however, when reached the Supreme Court later, was dealt with on an entirely different issue, *viz.* the recognition of foreign divorce decrees in India. The Supreme Court did not consider the vital issue of independent married women's domicile in cases of Court's jurisdiction in matrimonial cases.

Recently Supreme Court in *Y. Narasimha Rao* v. *Y. Venkata Lakshmi*[31] recommended the law under which parties were married as applicable law for dissolution of the marriage as well. According to the Court :"The jurisdiction assumed by the foreign Court as well as the grounds on which the relief is granted must be in accordance with the matrimonial law under which the parties are married".[32] In the opinion of the court this rule "frees them (women) from the bondage of the tyrannical and servile rule that wife's domicile follows that of her husband and that it is husband's domiciliary and law which determines the jurisdiction and judges the merits of the case."[33]

Thus this rule enunciated by the Supreme Court in this case has made the role of domicile irrelevant for the purposes of matrimonial jurisdiction from the view point of wife's position in India. However, the entire exercise will be fruitful only if the foreign court seized of the case decides to apply the rule evolved by the Indian Supreme Court.

The cases of deserted wives are on the increase and they have failed to make any mark on the Indian legislature. It may be pointed out that under these circumstances the Indian Law Commission[34] which has relentlessly been working towards providing lenient grounds and procedures for matrimonial causes in general and divorce in particular, is found to be wanting in dealing with situations caused by *Teja* v. *Satya* cases. In this context, there is no reason why India should not follow the example of other countries that protect women from being deserted and exploited. For example in U.S.A., U.K. and some European countries, a married woman can acquire domicile independent of her spouse.

The most significant aspect here is the jurisdiction of the courts in matrimonial matters. The very basis of this jurisdiction in almost all the countries is the domicile of the parties. Therefore, a remedy for a deserted wife's matrimonial cause may lie in the choice of the following two options. In the first option, the wife's domicile should be independent of her husband's domicile—in which case the matrimonial jurisdiction based on parties' domicile will not result in creating hardship to the wife to go to the court in her own right. This indeed is the situation in UK under the provisions of the Domicile and Matrimonial Proceedings Act, 1973.[35]

The second option concerns the changes introduced recently in the basis of the court's jurisdiction in matrimonial matters. For example, petitioner's residence has been considered as one of the basis for matrimonial jurisdiction. The 1976 Marriage Laws Amendment Act which amended Section 19 of the Hindu Marriage Act and Section 31 of the Special Marriage Act has now made it possible for the spouse to file his or her petition for relief in a matrimonial matter in the place of his or her residence.[36] It is submitted that while the English Act makes "habitual residence" as a base alternative to the parties' domicile, the Indian legislation is content with "residence", simpliciter. The mantle has fallen on the courts to qualify the same and bring on par with the situation in other countries like England. The notion of "habitual residence" is being followed in majority of the countries. The changes made in the Indian matrimonial legislation can bring about relief only partially, catering only the parties governed by these legislations. India being country with many personal laws that govern marital status needs a general change that would *ipso facto* bring about the necessary basic alterations in conflict aspects without depending upon the various minor changes that needs to be introduced in different personal laws individually. A major change in the basic policy will also bring about the Indian position on the same lines as those of other countries in matters of principle of private international law. Domicile conceptually forms the central theme in Private International Law. "Habitual residence" as a concept needs to be equated with "domicile". It should be made part of general law of the land to bring about the necessary solutions for many a problems that have been dealt with in this article.

NOTES AND REFERENCES

1. The word domicile derived from the Latin word "domus" meaning a dwelling house or home.
2. According to Blacks' Law Dictionary, domicile means "That place where a man has his true, fixed and permanent home and principal establishment, and to which whenever he is absent he has the intention of returning". Black's Law Dictionary, 3rd edition, 1933, p. 607.
3. This rule was applied in *Attorney General for Alberta* v. *Cook* (1926) A.C. 444 where relief was not granted although the wife had earlier been judicially separated from her husband.
4. (1895) A.C. 517.
5. Dicey, *Conflict of Laws,* (7th Edn., 1958), p. 119; Graveson, *Conflict of Laws,* (3rd Edn., 1955), p. 87. Read, H.E., *Recognition and Enforcement of Foreign Judgements* (1938), pp. 202-16; Willis, *Canadian Bar Review,* p. 7 and

Falconbridge, *Essays on the Conflict of Laws,* (2nd Edn., 1954), pp. 729-33. Martin Wolff described this rule: "When a valid marriage is concluded the wife immediately loses her domicile and acquires that of her husband and if later he changes his domicile she shares the new one. English law does not allow any exception to this rule. Even if the husband deserts her and established a domicile in a foreign country, or if the spouses are judicially separated, she acquires his domicile in countries to which she neither goes nor is bound to go". Wolff, Martin, *Private International Law,* (2nd Edn.), Oxford, 1950, pp. 120-21. See also in this connection *Warrender* v. *Warrender* (1935) 2 CI 89 Fin 488. *Attorney General for Alberta* v. *Cook* (1926), A.C. 444.

6. *Bater* v. *Bater* (1906), p. 209. *Stathos* v. *Stathos* (1993) p. 46, *Montaigu* v. *Montaigu* (1913), p. 154.
7. (1963), at 259.
8. *Ibid.*, at 267.
9. For further details see, Wolff, *Private International Law* (Oxford, 1950), 2nd Edn., at 120-22 and Palsson, Lennart, *Marriage and Divorce in Comparative Conflict of Laws* (Leiden, 1974), at 71-73.
10. Rober A. Leflar, *American Conflicts Law* (The Bobbs - Merrill Company, Inc., New York, 1968).
11. *The Law of Manu,* Chap. IX, V3, 328 (1964 reprint).
12. For more details on this aspect see Prof. T.S. Rama Rao, "Private International Law in India", *The Indian Year-book of International Affairs,* vol. IV, (1955), 219 at 234.
13. Section 15: By marriage a woman acquires the domicile of her husband if she had not the same domicile before.

    Section 16: A wife's domicile during her marriage follows the domicile of her husband.

    Exception: The wife's domicile no longer follows that of her husband if they are separated by the sentence of a competent Court, or if the husband is undergoing a sentence of transportation.

    It was held in *Kashiba* v. *Shripat,* (19 Bom. 697) by the Bombay High Court that the word "sentence" in Section 16 means both a decree of divorce and a decree for judicial seperation.
14. See Section 4 of the 1925 Act.
15. AIR 1946 Lah. 440.
16. *Ibid.*, at 442.
17. (1934) 59 Bom. 278 at 283.
18. AIR (1942) 2 Cal. 165.
19. AIR 1951 Pat. 454. In this case the wife who had gone to Pakistan at the time of partition, visited India after 3 years on a permit issued by the Indian High Commission.
20. AIR 1954 All. 457.
21. The Supreme Court in *State of Bihar* v. *Aman Singh* (AIR 1955 S.C. 282) in a similar factual situation held that the terms of Article 7 of the Indian Constitution (dealing with Migration) "clearly override Article 5". The S.C. however did not disagree "that her domicile was that of her husband".
22. AIR 1953 Cal. 530.
23. AIR 1959 Raj. 133.
24. See, T.S. Rama Rao's comment on this case in *The Indian Yearbook of International Affairs* (1960-61), vol. IX-X, at 170-2.

25. AIR 1965 J&K. 83.
26. ILR 1968 A.P. 101.
27. *Ibid.*, at 115.
28. See *Seetha Lakshmi Ammal* v. *Ponnuswamy Nadar* (1967) 2 MLJ 334; *Controller of Estate Duty* v. *Malnikoff* (1982) 134 ITR 583; and *Teja Singh v. Satya*, AIR 1971 P & H. 80.
29. AIR 1971 P & H. 80.
30. (1895) A.C. 517.
31. (1991)3 Sec 451. This case concerns with the recognition of foreign divorce decrees in India. The parties were married in India in accordace with Hindu Law. The husband obtained a divorce decree from the U.S. The wife remained *ex parte* to proceedings in the U.S. The S.C. refused recognition to the U.S. decree of dissolution of maarriage. See also for a discussion on this case, "Recognition of Foreign Divorce Decree in India : A case for Contextual Interpretation" by this author in 33 *JILI* 432 (1991) and also *ASI*, vol. XXVII (1991) 'Conflict of Laws' 493 at 508 and 509.
32. *Ibid* at 462.
33 *Ibid* & 463.
34. See 59th, 65th and 71st Law Commission Reports in general and particularly 65th Report.
35. S. 5(2)(a). Thus, the Courts in England can now, under this provision exercise jurisdiction "if either of the parties to the marriage is domiciled in England at the time when the proceedings, are commenced". See also, *Cheshire and North's Private International Law*, 11th Edn. by P.M. North and J.J. Fawcett (London, 1987), p. 627.
36. See, Prof. T.S. Rama Rao's, "Marriage in Indian Conflict of Laws; Some Recent Developments", *The Indian Yearbook of International Affairs*, 1980, p. 338.

CONCEPT OF MATRIMONIAL PROPERTY

*Dr Poonam Pradhan Saxena**

A woman's financial dependence on her husband in the Indian social set up and consequently her secondary status in the family is considered neither extraordinary nor peculiar, but quite natural and common. Ordinary customs of our society expect a man to establish a matrimonial home, being the wage earner and the woman to assume the domestic responsibilities. Her dedication in looking after the house, enables a man to go out free of tensions and responsibilities and earn a livelihood. While no exhaustive enumeration of the wife's duties within the house is possible, the husband is enjoined to maintain[1] his wife and the children of this wedlock. The term maintenance includes not merely food, clothes and residence,[2] but also things necessary for the comfort and status in which a person entitled to be maintained can reasonably be expected to live.[3]

This right of maintenance flows from the social and temporal relationship between the husband and the wife,[4] and is not a consideration for her housework. As, even where the husband abandons the wife,[5] or where she is living separately for some justifiable cause,[6] she retains her rights of maintenance.[7]

Under the classical Muslim law, the husband's obligation to maintain his wife depends on her being faithful to him and obeying his reasonable commands.[8] But he is not bound to maintain a wife who refuses herself to him or is otherwise disobedient.[9] An implication of these provisions is, that a woman who performs the total housework can yet be denied, even this right of maintenance if she is otherwise disobedient.

A house is run by the joint efforts of both the spouses. The husband working outside and bringing the money and the woman working inside the house and utilizing it. But while the money

* Lecturer, Law Faculty, Delhi University.

he earns belongs exclusively to him the monetary worth of a woman's contribution to the family economy is ignored completely.

A house therefore is an institution where the husband is the employer and the wife an employee, her job including looking after him and his entire family's needs, cooking food, washing utensils and clothes, cleaning the house, working in fields, milking the cows and looking after them, fetching water. Even the children of this wedlock belong to the father but the tasks of giving birth, and upbringing them is womanly. She may get medical facilities, but absolutely no leave from the household chores. The management of the house, though more tedious and laborious than an ordinary office job (involving usually the mental capabilities only) is unremunerative, reducing the status of a wife to that of an unpaid worker. Enshrining the ideals that a woman's greatest wealth lies in earning the satisfaction of her family members and winning their love and affection through selfless service and sacrifice, the Dharmashastras and the custodians of our society have been very conveniently and successfully befooling her, which she realises only when her dreams are shattered by the hammers of adverse times. In the end she remains the looser. If the husband throws her out of the house (and the action is complete) she cannot claim even a right to live in this house nor claim compensation for her life and career ruined for the sake of it.

Matrimonial discords in a family usually have no adverse repercussions on the husband's status, rights, residence and job. An alternative (though in no way an adequate substitute) can always be arranged on payment for keeping his house, but viewing it from a woman's angle changes the total scenario. Out on roads, without a roof, for two square meals, she has to prove to the satisfaction of the court, that for her expulsion, she herself was not responsible. Further, litigation and enforcement of rights, being time consuming processes, on being shown the door, a woman remains incapable to straightaway walk to the court and obtain relief. Her dependance on parents (who may not choose to back her) or some other parental relation is unfortunate. It is not therefore a traditional shyness which forces a woman to suffer in silence preventing from walking out on her husband, but a helplessness; an awareness of a stark reality of her being nowhere, once she leaves or is thrown out. An overnight transformation of her status from that of a *grahlakshmi* to that of a destitute woman, losing all her respect and running from pillar to post for justice is what becomes of her.

Economic emancipation is the most important part of the social emancipation of a woman. A woman having independent economic existence will not be susceptible to social oppression with that amount of ease, as a woman who has no independent economic existence[1.0] The best possible way of ensuring economic security to woman is to grant monetary recognition of her domestic work, better stated : "Home management".

This demand for recognition of wife's contribution in the way of housework is growing in many countries[1.1] The international conference on the status of women, held in Nairobi in 1985, also pointed out the need to recognise the economic value of a wife's contribution towards the family income through household work. Their main recommendation was the conferment of ownership rights in favour of the wife in the property of the husband during his life time.

The English law in this context is noteworthy. The contribution of the wife to the family income through domestic work and consequently her rights over the capital assets of the husband came up for consideration in many English cases, while ascertaining the property rights of the respective spouses in the event of their separation under law.

Until recently the courts had limited powers in regard to the capital assets. They could determine the property rights of the parties by altering ante-nuptial or post-nuptial settlements, but were incompetent to order a transfer of property from one to another or even award a lumpsum money until 1963. Financial provisions could be made by the courts only through maintenance to the wife, applying the standard 1/3rd rule.

If the matrimonial home stood in the name of the husband, it was taken to belong to him entirely, both in law and in equity. The wife did not get any proprietary interests in it even in cases where she helped him buy it. The money that she gave him for this purpose was regarded as gift, not recoverable by her in law.[12]

However by a long list of cases starting from in *re Roger's Question*[13] till *Hazell* v *Hazell*,[14] it has been held by the courts that if a wife contributes directly or indirectly in money or money's worth, to the initial deposit or to the mortgage instalments, she gets an interest proportionate to her contribution. In some cases it is a half share, in others less.

These courts never succeeded, however, in getting the wife a share in the house by reason of her contributions, other than financial contribution. The injustice to her became an apparent and a well admitted concern. Seven members of the Royal Commission on Marriage and Divorce[15] presided over by Lord Morten of Henryton said,

> "if on marriage, she gives up her paid work in order to devote herself to caring for her husband and children, it is an unwarrantable hardship when in consequence she finds herself in the end with nothing she can call her own."[16]

In 1965, Sir Jocelyn Simon, when he was President, used a telling metaphor,

> "The cock can feather the nest because he does not have to spend most of his time sitting on it."[17]

He went on to give reasons in an address which he gave to the law society,[18]

> "In the generality of marriages, the wife bears and rears the children and minds the home. She thereby frees her husband for his economic activities. Since it is her performance of her functions which enables the husband to perform his, she is in justice entitled to a share in its fruits."

But the courts had not been able to do justice to her. In April 1969, in *Pettitt* v *Pettitt*,[19] Lord Hodson said,

> "I do not myself see how one can correct the imbalance which may be found to exist in property rights as between the husband and wife without legislation"

In *Porter* v *Porter*,[20] Sachs LJ said,

> "the court must always take into account how long the marriage had lasted and to what extent the wife had rendered domestic services to the husband."[21]

In their Report on "Financial Provisions in Matrimonial Proceedings", the Law Commission also emphasised the importance of the domestic work and the need for its recognition, they said,

> "We recommend that in the exercise of the court's armoury of powers to order financial provisions, it should be directed to have regard to various criteria. Among these, there is one of outstanding importance in regard to the adjustment of property rights as between the spouses. This is the extent to which each has contributed to the welfare of the family, including not only contributions in money or money's worth (as in determination of rights to particular items of property) but also the contributions made (normally by the wife) in looking after the home and family. This should meet the strongest complaint made by married women and recognised as legitimate by the Morton Commission in 1955, namely, that the contribution which wives make towards the acquisitions of the family assets by performing their domestic chores, thereby releasing their husbands for gainful employment, is at present wholly ignored in determining their rights. Under our proposal this contribution would be a factor which the court would be specifically directed to take into account."[22]

The judicial recognition of the monetary worth of the wife's domestic work was finally accorded legislative recognition in 1970. The Matrimonial Proceedings and Properties Act, 1970, which was a reforming statute designed to facilitate the granting of ancillary relief in cases where marriages have been dissolved, provided for an even greater measure of reform by conferring on the courts a power to effect a transfer of the assets of the one to the other after divorce. It set out in section 5, various criteria, and expressly provided as one of criteria,

> ". . . the contributions made by each of the parties to the welfare of the family including any contribution made by looking after the home or caring for the family."[23]

Lord Denning J, deciding a case[24] under the Act, made the following important observations,

> "the wife who looks after the home and family, contributes as much to the family assets as the wife who goes out to

work. The one contributes in kind the other in money or money's worth. If the court comes to the conclusion that the home has been acquired and maintained by the joint efforts of both, then, when the marriage breaks down, it should be regarded as the joint property of both of them no matter in whose name it stands. Just as the wife who makes substantial money contributions usually gets a share, so should the wife who looks after the house and care for the family. . . ."[25]

Dismissing as irrelevant the fact that the wife in this case was equally responsible for the break up, he observed,

"There will be many cases in which a wife (though once considered guilty or blameworthy) will have cared for the home and looked after the family for many years. Is she to be deprived of the benefit otherwise to be accorded to her by sec. 5(1) (f) because she shares responsibilities for the breakdown with the husband ?"[26]

Sec. 5 of the Matrimonial Proceedings and Properties Act, 1970 was re-enacted in sec. 25 of the Matrimonial Causes Act, 1973 and remained unamended for over a decade. The Matrimonial and Family Proceedings Act, 1984, however re-enacted sec. 25 and enacted three basic principles, to be kept in mind while making financial adjustment after separation.[27]

With respect to the right of the wife to live in the house belonging exclusively to the husband, she was entitled to claim a right of occupation at common law not only by virtue of her right to her husband's consortium but also by virtue of her right to be maintained by him, for his duty to provide her with maintenance, is primarily discharged by providing her with a house.[28]

This common law position has been of little importance, since the spouses were given statutory right to occupy the matrimonial home by the Matrimonial Homes Act, 1967. This Act was extensively amended during the next 15 years and its provisions are now consolidated in the Matrimonial Homes Act, 1983. By sec. 1 (1) of the 1983 Act,

"Where one spouse is entitled to occupy a dwelling house by virtue of a beneficial estate or interest or contract or by virtue of any enactment giving him or her the right to remain in occupation and the other spouse is not so entitled . . . the spouse not so entitled shall have the following . . . rights of occupation,

a) If in occupation, a right not to be evicted or excluded from the dwelling house or any part thereof by the other spouse, except with the leave of the court given by an order of this section;

b) If not in occupation, a right with the leave of the court so given, to enter into and occupy the dwelling house.[29]

Where the wife is in sole occupation of the matrimonial home following a separation, the husband's attempts to evict her and realise his capital by selling the house came up for consideration in many cases, and the rule laid down was, that a deserted wife could enforce her common law right[30] to remain in the matrimonial home (of which her husband was the beneficial owner) not only against him but also against anyone claiming through him other than a bonafide purchaser for value of a legal or equitable estate or interest without notice of her claim.[31]

The legal position in India in this context is worth examination. The only law, according substantive rights to the wife in the property of her husband, by express provisions of unity of possession and community of interests of the property of both the spouses during marriage is the Portuguese Civil Code, 1867,[32] applicable generally[33] to the inhabitants[34] of the State of Goa, and the union territories of Daman and Diu.[35] It provides for two such types of contracts known as the ante-nuptial contracts[36] to be executed by the spouses prior to their marriage by way of a public deed.[37] These contracts are irrevocable and inalterable, after the solemnisation of the marriage,[38] and are without prejudice to the rights of inheritance and the general administration of the properties by the husband.[39]

The first contract provides for the community of assets between the spouses of all the properties and liabilities present as well as future,[40] while the second provides for the simple community of assets and liabilities acquired or incurred during the course of marriage.[41] These joint properties belong to both the spouses. Though general administration and management of these vests in the husband, he remains incapable to alienate it or otherwise dispose it of either by sale, gift or even by a testament without the consent of his wife.[42] In the event of dissolution of marriage by death or divorce, the entire property is split in two halves, one half being the share of each spouse.[43] Thus even where the wife is not earning a salary, she acquires an equal right in the property earned by her husband during the course of marriage.

These ante-nuptial contracts are a recognition of the relationship that marriage creates between the spouses; and also take into account the economic value of a wife's effort in running the house and assuming all domestic responsibilities thus freeing the husband for his avocation.

None of our personal laws, not even the secular Indian Succession Act, 1925, recognises this contribution of the wife to the family economy. The concept of community of interests and unity of possessions of the spouses, acquired and enjoyed during marriage, therefore, is still foreign to a majority of Indians.

In the socio-economic conditions prevailing in our country, what to say of a right of the wife, in the property of her husband during his life time; her rights even on his death are not secured. Though she is a primary heir[44] to her husband's estate in all the personal laws, the husband if he chooses, can deprive her completely under his will[45].

The question then arises, as to what is the position of the property of the husband and/or wife when the parties separate under law.

Sec. 27 of the Hindu Marriage Act. 1955, empowers the court to make such provisions, as it deems just and proper in respect of any property, which is presented jointly to the spouses at or about the time of marriage.[46] An application to this effect should be made by the concerned party before the termination of the proceedings. The rule provided in sec. 27 therefore, is confined only to properties presented at or about the time of marriage to the husband and the wife jointly and is also silent about the criteria to be kept in mind while effecting a distribution of the same. The court therefore, has no jurisdiction to pass orders in regard to any other property of the spouses whether acquired by them jointly or individually.[47] There is no similar provision under the Special Marriage Act, 1954. As suggested by Paras Diwan,

> "in our law, we should make a provision under which the court should have power to make arrangement for the settlement of the spousal property i.e. property of the spouses, acquired by them, jointly or individually, not merely in favour of either party or both parties, but also in favour of children ....."[48]

Under the Parsi Marriage and Divorce Act, 1936, the provision of sec. 42 are identical to those of sec. 27 of the HMA, 1955.

The Indian Divorce Act, 1869, which till today remains the most controversial and orthodox piece of legislation, provides (at the time of separation), for the settlement of wife's property (by way of forfeiture of her rights) in favour of her husband and children. Sec. 39 provides.

> "Whenever the court pronounces a decree of dissolution of marriage or judicial separation for adultery of the wife, if it is made to appear to the court that the wife is entitled to any property, the court may, if it thinks fit, order such settlement as it thinks reasonable to be made of such property or any part thereof, for the benefit of the husband, or of the children of the marriage or of both."

The law in India in this respect, therefore, is far from satisfactory. As India cannot truly develop without the economic emancipation of woman, an urgent need is to recognise the economic value of her contribution towards family income through household work. The best possible way to achieve it, will be to confer on the wife ownership rights in the family asserts acquired during the subsistence of the marriage. The phrase 'family assets' is a convenient short way of expressing an important concept. It refers to those things which are acquired by one or other or both of the parties, with the intention that they should be continuing provisions for them and their children during their joint lives and used for the benefit of the family as a whole. The family assets can be divided into two parts.

i) those which are of a capital nature such as matrimonial home and the furniture in it, and,

ii) those which are of revenue producing nature, such as earning power of the husband or wife.[49]

On their separation under law, the capital assets should be split in two halves, each spouse taking a moiety of the total property. When either party dies, the half of it should immediately vest in the surviving spouse, the other half going by succession. During the subsistence of the marriage, none of the spouses should be allowed to dispose it of without the consent of the other.

There is an apprehension, that, this recommendation, though meritorious in substance, is so alien to the Indian society even in the changed social structure of today that its acceptance will be difficult. A move to register the houses allotted and sold by the Delhi Development Authority in the joint names of the spouses was opposed by women themselves (majority of them being victims of matrimonial discord) as they did not want the flat bought by their hardearned money to belong automatically to their husbands also.

It is a well known fact that in some of the western countries, housekeeping is a fully paid professional job. Accordingly, it may be suggested in the alternative, that for according justice to a woman without straining the cordial and harmonious relations of the family, a proper approach can be a direct recognition of the monetary worth of her domestic work; its evaluation in terms of money; a fixed monthly allowance analogous to a salary which may or may not be strictly called an incentive but should be an adequate compensation for her work. She should not be made to regret the fact that she wasted her career for the sake of her family. For calculating this monthly allowance areawise committees should be set up (comprising of responsible persons). This allowance should be separate and not a part of household expenditure, to be spent on the house. Where either she is not paid regularly or allows her husband to keep it, it should remain her property in his custody and should not be treated as her relinquishment. On their separation, she must be paid the entire amount, calculated till the last day she lived and worked in his house, even where she is proved to be guilty of a matrimonial misconduct (because no rule in any department allows a forfeiture of the salary of an employee for a period where he has actually worked, even though later he is dismissed on corruption charges). Where the husband files a matrimonial proceeding against his wife and errs in making the payment of the domestic allowance, his defence should be struck down. Where a woman works both outside and inside the house, without any prejudice to the salary she draws her claim to the domestic allowance must withstand. An implementation of these recommendations will act as a deterrent in way of hasty separations and will go a long way[50] in solving economic problems of women. Our legislature's concern about bonded slavery, bonded, labours, and unequal payment to women outside their homes was apparent. There is no reason why it should not equally be concerned, about a woman being in fact a bonded labour inside her house. It is time when she should be given her right and privileges in law, of which she has been robbed. The injustice perpetrated on her in the name of duty should be remedied and her work should be honoured. That will be a real homage to our constitutional principles.

NOTES AND REFERENCES

1. This duty of maintaining one's wife and children has been described as a 'burden' by S.S. Sandeawalia J in *Kailashwati* v. *Ajodhia Parkash*, 1977(79) P.L.R. 216 see. para 19.
2. *Charandas* v. *Nagubai*, (1929) B. 452; 31 Bom. L.R. 1128 *Parwatibai* v. *Sadoo*, (1941) N.L.J. 571. *Thulsai* v. *Raghavan*, AIR (1985) Ker, 20.
3. *Srinivas* v *Lakshmi*, AIR (1928) Mad. 216.
4. N.V. Ragdhavachariar, "*Hindu Law, Principles and Precedent*" 7th Ed, Ed. by S. Venkataraman (1980) p. 215
   See also *Laxmi Devi* v. *Nagama*, AIR (1925) Mad. 757;
   Rattamma v. *Seshachalam*, AIR (1927) Mad. 502;
   Bai Appitbai v. *Khimji*, AIR (1936) Bom. 138;
   Udayanath v. *Siridei*, AIR (1973) Ori. 196.
5. *Laxmi Sahuani* v. *Maheswar Sahu* (1985) (2) H.L.R. 283 (Orissa).
6. *Gajendra* v. *Sulochana*, 68 C.L.J. 559
7. See, Sec. 18, The Hindu Adoptions and Maintenance Act, 1956.
8. Mulla,'*Principles of Mahomedan Law*'. 18th Ed., by M. Hidayatullah and Arshad Hidayatullah (1977). p. 300;
9. *A* v. *B*, (1896) 21 Hom 77 at p. 82;
   Mt. Khatiyan v. *Abdullah*, AIR (1942) Ker. 535.
10. Shri Sadhan Gupta, Lok Sabha Debates, Part 2 vol. IV (1955), p. 8053.
11. Report of the committee on '*Status of Women in India*' 1973; p. 141.
12. *Balfour* v. *Balfour*, (1919) 2 K.B. 571.
13. (1948) 1. All E.R. 328.
14. (1972) 1. W.L.R. 301.
15. Commissioned (9678) in 1956.
16. Id at p. 178.
17. See. (1970) A.C. 77, at 811.

18. (1965) 62 Law Society Gazette, 345.
19. (1970) A.C 777, 811.
20. (1969) 1. W.L.R. 115.
21. Id at p. 116.
22. Law Commission No. 25, H of C (1968-69), No. 448 p. 34, para 69.
23. See 5 (1) (f), the Matrimonial Proceeding and Properties Act, 1970.
24. *Wachtel* v *Wachtel*, (1973) 2. W.L.R. 366.
25. Id at p. 376.
26. Id at p. 372.
27. These three principles are ;
    i) removal of the status quo-ideal or minimum loss principle
    ii) giving priority to the welfare of any child of the family; and
    iii) placing greater emphasis on the parties becoming self sufficient.
    see P. Brombley, *'Family Law'*, 7th Ed., by P.M.Bromley and N.V.Lowe,London (1987) p. 679-680.
28. *Price* v. *Price*, (1951) 1 ALLER, p. 413 at p. 420-421.
    W v *W* (1954) 2, ALLER 829, at 840.
29. See S. 10(1), dwelling home, has been defined as including any building or part of a building occupied as a dwelling together with any yard, garden, garage or outhouse belonging to it and occupied with it. See *Kinzler* v *Kinzler*, (1985) Family Law 26. C.R.
30. Popularly called a deserted wife's equity.
31. See P. Bromley—*'Family Law'*, 7th Ed, by P.M. Bromley and N.V.Lawe, London (1987) p. 548.
32. The Portuguese Civil code, 1867, which was enforced in Portugal in 1868 was extended to its overseas provinces including Goa, Daman and Diu with effect from 1870. (See art. 9).
33. P.M.S. Usgaocar, Family laws in Goa, Daman and Diu; 'Are they Uniform' in *'Family laws in Goa'* Ed., Sardesai (1982) p. 64-71.
34. See. Art 5, The Portuguese Civil Code, 1867. In 1961, Goa was liberated and in the following year, the Constitution of India was amended. In 1962 itself, the legislation affecting Goa, namely the Goa, Daman and Diu (Administration) Act, 1962 was passed. See Sec. 5 (1) of the Act.
35. As early as 1880, the Portuguese has protected some Hindu usages and customs relating to marriage, adoption, and joint family for the Hindus of Goa, Daman and Diu. In its application to local Hindus, the Portuguese laws have been subjected to the provisions of these protective laws. See Code of Usages and Customs of the non-Christians Inhabitants of Daman, 1854;
    Decrees of Usages and Customs of Gentile Hindus of Goa, 1880. Usages and Customs of non-Christians inhabitants of Diu, 1894. See also, T. Mahmood, *'Studies in Hindu law'* (1981) p. 64.
36. See the Portuguese Civil Code, 1867, Arts, 1096, 1098-1110.
37. Id., Art 1097.
38. Id ., Art 1106.
39. Id ., Art 1104.
40. Id ., Art 1109.
41. Id., Art 1125, 1131-1133.
42. Id., Art 1119.
43. Id., Art 1123; see also Gopal Apa Kamat, Family laws in Goa, Daman and

Diu, are they uniform, in *"Glimpses of Family law in Goa, Daman and Diu"*, Ed., Sardesai (1982) p. 64-71.

44. See The Hindu succession Act, 1956, Secs. 8-13, Sec.17, and the schedule, Decree of Usages and Customs of the Gentile Hindus of Goa, 1880, Arts. 24, Code of Usages and Customs of non Christians Inhabitants of Daman, 1854; Arts. 50, 53, 54, Code of Usages and Customs of non-Christian inhabitants of Diu, 1894; Arts. 33, 34, 35 *E.Kinbabee* v. *Ashruf Ali*, (1864) I.W.R. 152; Tyabji *'Mohammedan Law'* (4th Ed., by Mushsin Tyabji) (1985) p. 847; P. Diwan, *'Muslim Law in Modern India'*, 3rd Ed., (1985) p. 208; The Indian Succession Act, 1925. Secs. 33, Secs. 54.

45. Except under the Islamic law, a person has unfettered testamentary powers under all other personal laws. See, The Hindu Succession Act, 1956, Sec. 30.
The Indian Succession Act, 1925. Sec. 51.
Paras Diwan, "Muslim Law in Modern India",
3rd Edn., (1985) p. 214.
Ballie, 'Digest of Moohamedan Law,' Part 1 (1963) p. 117.

46. See The Hindu Marriage Act, 1955, Sec 27 provides,
"In any proceedings under this Act, the court may make such provisions in the decree as it deems just and proper with respect to any property presented at or about the time of marriage which may belong jointly to both the husband and the wife."

47. *S.S. Singh* v *Manjeet*, (1983) J&K 86.

48. Paras Dewan, *'Modern Hindu Law'*, 7th Ed; (1988), p. 194.

49. *Watchel* v. *Watchal*, (1973) 2. W.L.R. 366, at 373.

50. After staying and working for 43 years in the house of her husband, Shah Bano was divorced, and after paying her maintenance for three months, her husband washed his hands off her. After being on roads for 3 years, she filed a petition for maintenance, which again was decided 7 years later. See *Mohd. Ahmed Khan* v. *Shah Bano Begum*. AIR (1985) SC 945. If according to the suggestion, the husband was made to pay per month a sum of her calculated till the time of showing her the door, would he have dared to treat her as he did and would she indeed have been a helpless woman which she had become?

INDIAN WOMEN : VICTIMS OF THE INDIAN CONSTITUTION

*Krishan Mahajan**

A revolution in India has gone almost unnoticed. It is a book called the Constitution of India. The book governs every Indian regardless of religion, caste, language, locality or political belonging. For the first time in India's history a secular book governs religion, caste, language, politics, economy, science and all government. This book defines what kind of India we must have. It is this book by virtue of which there is a country called India and there is a government, legislature, courts, the police and the armed forces. It is this book that promises justice (social, economic and political), liberty, equality and fraternity for all Indian citizens regardless of whether they are men or women. However, these stirring aims of this book have been worked out in a contradictory manner. These are the fundamental contradictions of the Indian State. It is essential to understand these before one talks of justice, equality and fraternity for Indian women since these constitute the first legal constraint for women in their access to justice. These contradictions deny them access to justice at the very threshold.

In India women exist generally, if not only, either as part of their parent's home or of their husband's home. Justice, liberty and equality for her depend on the condition of these families. Since the condition of most Indian families is one of utter poverty and illiteracy, that automatically defines the existence of most Indian women. This means that a large number of women who are a part of the bonded labour families must never get justice since their families do not get justice, even though the

*Law Editor of The Indian Express, a weekly legal columnist and a specialist on law and development.

Supreme Court has expanded the constitutional prohibition against bonded labour to cover those cases where less than the prescribed minimum wages are paid.[1] This situation arises directly because of the first constitutional contradiction between the fundamental right of not being forced into labour and the mere directive principle of State Policy preventing such labour out of "economic necessity".[2]

The Indian Constitution recognised the prevalence of bonded labour and declared that forced labour is prohibited and went further to declare it as an offence. It made this into a fundamental right enforceable by approaching the Supreme Court directly. Today this right can be enforced by a letter to the highest court or a high court.[3]

And now the contradiction. The prevention of "economic necessity" which causes bonded labour or the acceptance of work at less than the prescribed minimum wages has been made by this very Constitution a non-enforceable right. This became part of the bundle of social justice rights called directive principles; which though declared to be fundamental in the governance of the country cannot be enforced through any court.[4] The same applies to fundamental duties[5] which require every Indian to renounce practices derogatory to women, since unlike the fundamental rights chapter in the Constitution there is no statement in the chapter on Fundamental Duties that the right to enforce these duties is a fundamental right.

This seals the fate of women who in a bonded labour's family, whether parental or matrimonial, constitute the most vulnerable section vis-a-vis the contractor or the landlord and law-enforcing agencies like the police. Yet the women, twice structured, once in the family and then in the family which is in bondage, must for her liberation complain to the police under the Bonded Labour Abolition Act. Even if she complains to the district magistrate she must be ready to face the police[6] who alone will investigate the offence and collect the evidence against probably the most powerful economic person in the area and also the sole provider of jobs.

This contradiction operates against women right from childhood. It is a fundamental right of a child below fourteen not to be engaged in any factory, mine or any hazardous employment.[7] But their right not to enter avocations unsuited to their age or strength because of "economic necessity" is a non-enforceable directive principle.[8] Yet economic necessity leaves Indian women with only two choices : to either be protected by their family by playing subsidiary non-monetary roles of helping their menfolk at work or in the home; or in the alternative to put themselves up in the marketplace as prostitutes. In the first case they are the victims of all the rights essential to their dignity but unenforceable : free compulsory primary education[9], the right to special care of the educational and economic interests of the weaker sections especially of the scheduled castes and scheduled tribes,[10] the right to an adequate nutrition and the right to have childhood and youth protected against exploitation.[11] The right to work and public assistance against "undeserved want" is not only unenforceable but subject to the 'Limits of the economic capacity and development' of India.[12] In the second case the illiterate, unskilled and destitute girl child sells the only thing relevant to the male market—her body, because the right to have childhood protected against moral and material abandonment is again an unenforceable right.

This is a fundamental pattern of our fundamental document called the Constitution. All adverse results are prohibited and enforceable—like child labour, forced labour, untouchability, or generally arbitrary official action especially concerning trade business, occupation, speech, movement or association. But all the causes which lead to the specific evils prohibited or facilities which would enable people to resist official or private arbitrariness, are not enforceable. Negative laws concerned only with the prevention of evil results are enforceable and positive laws for preventing these results are not enforceable. The Constitution makes the Indian State unaccountable to any forum. It shackles Indian families and their women by denying them access to the constitutionally promised justice[13]—social, economic and political—by simply denying them the right to enforce these rights in the courts or in any forum.

The Supreme Court has contributed its own share to the inbuilt injustice in the Constitution. These vital but unenforceable social rights called directive principles are now implemented through a host of administrative schemes and guidelines. The Supreme Court has declared that these schemes and guidelines are not necessarily 'law'. This puts the poor out of the court in terms of enforcing their fundamental rights against these schemes or guidelines, since under the fundamental rights chapter only a 'law' can be challenged. Since there is no other forum where the administration can be held accountable the highest court only adds to the unaccountability. Even when bonded labour goes to the highest court it gets grand judgements but no real freedom. A typical example is the *Bandhua Mukti Morcha* case in which for the last five years the highest court has not said a single word on the detailed and probably the first environment integrated rehabilitation plan put before it for the 10,000 Faridabad quarry workers.[14]

The second constraint in terms of access of justice for women is the Supreme Court itself which has built no model of planning research and monitoring[15] social justice cases or even to give priority to them in terms of court time.

This is not to decry the useful role that the court performs as a check against the worst kind of atrocities. This is just to underline the functioning of the court as an agency against the worst abuse instead of a positive agency of social justice. With the number of bonded labour cases it has handled one would have expected it to formulate by now standard inputs for rehabilitation which is a mandatory requirement under the Bonded Labour Abolition Act. Yet that has not been done.

In city slums or rural urban areas where women labour as home workers the labour machinery is such as to deny access to justice for such women. The labour machinery is understaffed qualitatively and quantitatively and the labour secretary's job has no dependence on any index of achievement for the labour he is supposed to look after. Whether it is *bidi* rollers[16], *chikan* workers[17] or ready made garment workers[18] our field studies have shown that inspite of specific laws as in the case of *bidi* workers, the labour enforcement machinery simply does not treat the women workers as its protective subjects. Almost all labour inspectors and officers are fighting their own battles of seniority between direct recruits and promotees as also transfers. There is today a serious problem of women vendors versus the police licensing system for hawkers and it seems that the Police Commissioner system serves interests other than those of the people.[19]

The Constitution, the Supreme Court, the labour enforcement machinery and the police are the obstacles to women's access to economic justice – the sole base for women's freedom. We have so far referred to one aspect of economic justice, that is, a fair return for their labour. But our legal system which has to be 'socialist' under the Constitution also provides for redistribution of the most basic asset of a developing country, namely land. But the triangle of land reform, people's participation through panchayati raj and cooperatives has been broken and politicised to an extent that land reform all alone limps along. The socialist laws on land reforms have had two effects. One, poor families who have no knowledge of these laws have learnt about them when they found the estate manager or the landlord suddenly descending to deprive them of their status as tenants or labourers with homesteads. Legally tenant families were reduced to labourers or servants and labourers on the farm found themselves ousted to join the realm of the landless and the bonded. This reduced the women in such families to further poverty. Second, because of the land ceiling law many of the wives of landlords and estate managers found themselves legally divorced so that the family could hold onto more land since the woman as an individual unit is entitled to more land but not as a wife, who merges into the definition of 'family'.[20] This finds its parallel in the city where educated women lend their names to the business of their husbands for purposes of tax evasion.[21] So a socialist law in the context of its operation, that is a non-socialist State economic policy, can only work to the detriment of women by denying them economic justice.[22]

The same applies to the entire sector of handlooms and handicrafts, the largest sector of employment after agriculture. Under the State Zila Parishad Acts and Panchayati Acts women are to have token representation on the committees meant to discharge the mandatory duty of district collectors to develop and finance these handicrafts by surveying them, procuring raw materials, training people and marketing the products. They also have token representation under the Acts like those concerning *bidi* workers. But one simply finds the wrong kind of women representing women, which throws up a whole new dimension of *women* versus *women* or women denying women access to justice.[23]

Lastly we come to the whole area of matrimony and a woman passing into another family. At the outset one would like to distinguish between the educated minority of women and the rest. When the educated minority gets married with dowry and goes in for amniocentesis and abortions they have only themselves to blame. In the questionable legislative trend of the criminalisation of offences against women (dowry, cruelty, death within seven years of marriage) one finds that post marital complaints of dowry suddenly emerge when such women are at the receiving end.

But a more serious problem lurks for the majority of the illiterate women kept in poverty. This is the fundamental constitutional contradiction between the recognition of 'custom or usage' as a source of law in Article 13 of the Fundamental Rights chapter and the requirement that every Indian government must endeavour to have a uniform civil code in the directive principles. Thus custom, which fragments Indian women almost tehsil to tehsil, is enforceable in courts but not the need for a uniform civil code which would create legally one Indian woman. Like the word 'raid' (the legal word is only search) politicians and the unthinking media have foisted on the public mind the word 'personal laws'. The word 'personal law' does not exist anywhere in the Constitution. All that exists under Article 372 is law in existence before the constitution. Even such laws, including custom, cannot violate fundamental rights and if they do they are liable to be struck down by virtue of Article 13. This is so because Article 15 clearly prohibits any Indian government from discriminating against anybody only on the grounds of religion. Even the fundamental right in Article 25, the freedom to practice profess or propagate a religion, is specifically made subject to another Article apart from being subjected to public order, health morality and the other fundamental rights. Yet legally today women are defined for purposes of matrimony adoption and succession as Hindu, Muslim, Christian, Parsi, Jew, Sikh and others.[24] There is no such thing as an Indian woman in Indian family and succession law. This legal fragmentation of Indian women not only thwarts the Constitution but strengthens the hold of religion on the mind of women and thereby distances them from the only concept of justice permitted to be recognised—that is the Constitution.

The question that logically follows is why does this happen? There are at least three reasons for this. One our information system, including education, which formulates attitudes. We have no TV programme, newspaper campaign[25] or duty cast on State PROs to transmit constitutional values to the people so that these would replace other values. The second and most crucial probably is unconstitutional economic policy and planning.[26] The Constitution requires as a fundamental of governance that all investment, technology and revenue policy or planning be informed by social justice as defined in the directive principles. The Planning Commission, the Finance, Human Resource, Industry and Commerce Ministries have not even evolved a machinery to test their policies on this constitutional mandate. That alone explains the separate compartmentalised approaches to child labour and women. In technical jargon, children, women and social justice as defined in the Constitution (including environment) are costs not investments, "externalities" to economic planning not integrated parts thereof. The third reason is the failure of all political parties and the learned class to demand a constitutional orientation of the Indian economy. The most used constitutional weapon in India's polity has been the Governor's report to the Union Government on the constitutional breakdown of a State government and its replacement by Central rule. Yet none of the learned elite have ever demanded that the Governor report regularly on the implementation of social justice in his State and report constitutional breakdown on such grounds. Till we create and mobilise opinion towards these issues, fragmented Indian women must keep on suffering in silence while a handful of educated women continue to waste their time in crime against women cells or criminal courts.[27]

NOTES AND REFERENCES

1. *Bandhua Mukti Morcha* v. *Union of India* 1984 (2) SCR 67 and *Neerja Chaudhary* v. *State of M.P* (1984) 3 SCC 243—While the Supreme Court, instead of the Government and Parliament, sets the national verbal agenda on socio-economic justice, it has not evolved any machinery for informing the vast illiterate poulation of this agenda or for monitoring its implementation or building up its legal aid programme for its execution.
2. Articles 23 & 39 (e).
3. *S.P. Gupta* v. *U.O.I.* 1982 (2) SCR at 520.
4. Art. 37.
5. Art. 51 A.
6. Sec. 22 of the Act makes the offence cognisable. Yet no case has ever been registered against a district magistrate who under section 12 is bound to trace out and rehabilitate bonded labour in his district.
7. Art. 24.
8. Art. 29(e).
9. Art. 45.
10. Art. 46.
11. Art. 41—The recent movement of the Supreme Court in *K.P.J. Unnikrishnan* or the Capitation fee case, to enforce Directive Principles by reading these

into fundamental rights, is rather shaky. Primary education, a key input for women, is a fundamental right under this judgement but with no machinery (Art. 39-A) for its implementation. In post-school or higher education the court has not said that it will examine whether ruling politicians under Article 41 are provided education within the "limits of economic capacity and development" of the State.

13. Preamble to the Constitution.
14. K. Mahajan with Dr. Patwardhan *Constitution, Environment and Bonded Labour : The case of Faridabad Stone Quarry Workers.* Report submitted to the Supreme Court as a Law Expert, 1984.
15. *Planning Research and Monitoring Plan for Public Interest Litigation in the Supreme Court of India,* K. Mahajan, Report Submitted to the Chief Justice of India, Mr. Justice P.M. Bhagwati, 1985.
16.. K. Mahajan, *Socio-Legal Study of Women Bidi-workers in Gujarat* (Gujarat, SEWA, 1986).
17. K. Mahajan, *Socio-Legal Crisis of Chikan Embroidery Women Workers of Lucknow* (Gujarat, SEWA, 1988).
18. K. Mahajan, *The Legal Alternatives for Ready Made Garment Women Workers of Gujarat* (Gujarat, SEWA, 1988).
19. See the Supreme Court Judgement in the Ahmedabad Women Vegetable Hawkers case.
20. K. Mahajan, "Land Reforms : A planned failure in Law and Social Change" in J.S. Gandhi ed., 1987, *Sociological Congress Proceedings.*
21. K. Mahajan, "Operation of the Agricultural Land Ceiling Act" in Bihar, 1987 in J.S. Gandhi ed. *Sociological Congress Proceedings.*
22. Dr. V. Gaurishankar, "Women and Tax" Paper presented at Women's Development Cell Workshop on Women in the Indian Family, Lady Shri Ram College, 1987.
23. K. Mahajan with Prof. Upendra Baxi, Socio-Legal Study for the Supreme Court on the Leather workers in the Kanpur Zila Parishad, Supreme Court of India, 1985.
24. See the Special Marriage Act 1954 which has been amended to protect property rights of those who marry under this Act. This economically pushes the Act back into the separate religious identity of Indian women.
25. The press owners and editors will have a whole team to cover Parliament or sports but will not appoint a full time correspondent duly qualified to cover the courts which decide the legality of what Parliament enacts. They will pay for Khushwant Singh's titillating journalism but will not pay for any popular legal column.
26. See K. Mahajan 'Law Development and Unconstitutional Economics' in Upendra Baxi ed. *Law and Poverty,* Upendra Baxi (Delhi, Bar Council of India, 1988).
27. K. Mahajan "An Alternative Legal Aid Plan for India", in P.K. Gandhi ed. *Public Interest Litigation,* (Delhi, Jamia Millia University, 1985), and "Legal Aid for 2000 A.D."—a report on the future of the Supreme Court Legal Aid Committee.

RESTITUTION OF CONJUGAL RIGHTS : A MISUSED LEGAL PROVISION

*Devinder Raheja**

Introduction

Existence of conjugal relations between the spouses is one of the cardinal bases of the married state. Conjugal relations imply, the living together of husband and wife, in the company and society of each other. Section 9 of the HMA[1] envisages to restore through judicial process, conjugal relations between the estranged spouses.

According to the section, "a deserted" or "abandoned" spouse is entitled to make an application to the court for the conjugal company of the other. The court "on being satisfied with the truth of the statement"[2] and in the absence of a "legal ground" against such "application" may decree the desired relief. An application for restitution, therefore, is a prayer to seek restoration of matrimonial relations through court order. However, the efficacy of a judicial pronouncement to normalise human relations, which the matrimonial relations are, is questionable. Justice P.A. Chaudary[3] has no misgivings in labelling the RCR[4] decree as "state coercion."[5] He convincingly observes that "it can neither prolong nor preserve the voluntary union of husband and wife." His observations that it can neither "soften the ruffled feelings nor clear the misunderstandings between the parties,"[6] need to be examined. An in-depth study of reported cases has been undertaken to discuss closely the pattern and operation of restitution orders and their effect on (1) the stability of marriage and (2) interests of spouses, more particularly that of the wife.

An examination of reported cases on matrimonial litigation unfolds that restitution petitions under S. 9 of the HMA find

*Senior fellow Nehru Memorial Meseum & Library, Teen Murti, New Delhi.

much favour with the litigants. Interestingly enough, a substantial number of the petitions are moved by the husband. Though the petition can be made by the husband as well as by the wife, cases reveal that only in a very few cases the wife has taken recourse to this matrimonial remedy. This pattern calls for a closer scrutiny of the operation of this legal remedy.

The thrust of the study is to examine with the aid of in-depth case study the circumstances of matrmonial home and conduct of the spouses leading to a petition for RCR. This insight would help evaluate whether a RCR decree is capable of fulfilling its avowed objective of restoring conjugal relations? (2) Whether the court while deciding cases takes into account the facts of matrimonial home and whether these judgments are socially relevant? (3) Whether the provision of restitution should continue to be a part of the Hindu Marriage Act, 1955? (4) Whether the 1964 amendment of S. 9 is conducive to the interests of the society?

Wife's Service and Use of Restitution Petition for Ulterior Motives

Husband's secured economic state and privileged social position prompts him to use this legal process for spurious motives. Restitution petition against a wife serving at another place, or who was made to leave the matrimomial home or who was abandoned; or a restitution petition following wife's maintenance application makes one suspect that the object prompting a restitution petition may not be to seek wife's company but rather the nefarious design of rejecting her in situations not allowed by the law.

A string of restitution petitions against a wife serving at a place different from that of the husband's lend an insight into the helpless state to which a wife can be driven to when the husband whimsically flings on her the ultimatum to resign and join him (which she may be reluctant to because of his cruel treatment) or to face an eventual divorce. In spite of the professed legal equality, some of the courts have upheld husband's unquestionable privilege of being the lord and master. Many a court, in such cases had succumbed to the temptation of vindicating the ancient supremacy of the husband over his wife, and the result was that unmindful of the facts of the case before them, or the economic compulsions of the present-day society, wife's living at a place different from that of the husband because of her job was not interpreted as a 'reasonable excuse.'[7] This narrow and orthodox interpretation of the section enabled many a husband to get the decree of restitution which was used as a spring-board for an eventual divorce. A perusal of such cases reveals that the singular intention for securing the decree has been to oppress the wife by making her resign her job or to get rid of her.

The fact and circumstances of *Pillalamarri Vara Prasad* v. *Pillalamarri Seshalakshmi*,[8] testify the above said assertion. Because of husband's insistence to resign, the wife took leave and promised to resign when her life with him 'gets adjusted and runs smoothly"[9] but the husband instead brought a restitution petition. The wife's contention was that the restitution petition was made "to make her helpless and utterly dependent so that she would be completely at the mercy of the husband to be abused and beaten."[10] However, unmindful of the facts and wife's predicament, the court gave a narrow construction to S. 9(2) and upheld husband's stand by observing "under Hindu law it is the duty of the wife to live with her husband . . . employment in service at another place and the very insistence . . . and refusal to resign . . . amounts to withdrawal from society without sufficient cause."[11] The case of *Gaya Prasad* v. *Smt. Bhagwati*[12] again shows judicial insensitivity to the wife's helpless condition. The wife's allegation was that due to adverse financial circumstances she was forced to take up a job. Later, her husband not only whimsically insisted on her leaving the job but he also "threatened to cut her nose" and tried to take her away with the help of goondas. In her pleadings as well as in her testimony before the court, she expressed her willingness to consort with the husband. Bhargava J. of the Madhya Pradesh High Court, ignored the findings of the trial court and held that she could continue her service only "by mutual consent and concurrence."[13] Wife's deposition that she "apprehended danger to her life from him," was interpreted by the honourable court as *animus deserendi* and the husband was granted the petition because "small income" of the husband, in the opinion of the court was not a "sufficient reason" to deny "wife's society to the husband." The judgment of this case was influenced by the reasoning of a prior Punjab case.[14] Therein too, the relief of restitution was allowed to be used as a weapon by the husband for his designs. With a view to get a job, at her husband's persuasion, the wife went in for a tailoring diploma. She got a job at another town. Facts reveal that conjugal relations subsisted between the spouses and the wife used to send money to her husband and her father-in-law. However, when she refused to pay all the demanded amount the husband quarrelled with her and demanded her to resign. On wife's refusal to toe his line he came up with the restitution petition. Though the wife through her letter to the husband and in her deposition before the court expressed her desire to continue with the marriage alongwith the job, Justice A.N. Grover felt that she could not "be allowed to virtually withdraw herself from the society of the husband in this manner"[15] who, the court observed could not be required to "content himself by visiting the wife... or by her coming to live with him occasionally."[16] Similar stand was reaffirmed in *Kailashwati* v. *Ayodhya Parkash.*[17] Unfortunately, these judgments had the effect of prescribing and limiting for the wife even in these years of professed equality, only a domestic and dependent role, howsoever miserable it might be to her.

"Undue attachment" to the "Hindu wife's duty of obedience and devotion to the husbabnd" and a total lack of comprehension as to the meaning of the word "cohabitation"[18] is reflected in these judgments. In none of the above mentioned cases it may be noted, the wife refused cohabitation with the husband. In fact, in *Tirath Kaur's*[19] case the husband was virtually cohabiting with her about the time he presented his petition. Hence, it was not the absence of cohabitation an obligation implicit in marital realtions, but husband's frustrations due to his failure in extorting money from his wife which made him rush to the court with a restitution petition. Under the circumstances, restitution petition was made not to have her company, but to reject her and to teach her a lesson. In the Andhra Pradesh[20] case, the wife promised to resign provided she was free from fears of being beaten and abused. In the Madhya Pradesh[21] case too, the wife was agreeable to consortium but for husband's threats of chopping of her nose and his coercion. Above mentioned cases are just tip of an iceberg revealing pitiable and horrendous conditions of women who are trapped in bad marriages. One wishes that at least the law should not have worsened their already miserable conditions through adverse interpretations which are neither warranted by law[22] nor facts of the cases.

A restitution decree creates a precarious situation for the wife who has either to opt out of economic independence or face the curse of divorce. Her predicament especially in a very miserable marriage is extremely traumatic to her. In none of the reported cases, the facts reveal, the wife had expressed priority of job over marriage. It was the bad marriage or economic compulsions which were the prime considerations for her reluctance in giving up the job at the insistence of her husbnd. The facts of *N.R. Radhakrishnan* v. *N. Dhanalakshmi*[23] also stand testimony to the above theses.

The husband, a driver, got himself transferred to spite his wife and asked her to resign, failing which he presented a petition for restitution. The wife alleged that in order to get her ornaments, husband gave her beatings. After scanning the facts, the court resolved that wife's withdrawal was "merely physical" and was "without the least intention of denying to her husband her society and company."[24]

In *Mirchumal* v. *Devi Bai,*[25] the wife who was serving prior to marriage resigned her job in favour of conjugal bliss, but unable to tolerate husband's illicit relations with another lady, coupled with her mother-in-law's cruelty, she procured an employment for herself. Denying restitution decree to the husband, the court observed, "compelling wife to leave her job would mean inequality before law and serious infringement of her fundamental rights."[26] The court rightly observed that as long as the wife does not snap her realtions with the husband and does not deny him access," the husband is not entitled to the decree. In *S. Garg* v. *K.M. Garg,*[27] the wife's rights were upheld on the anvil of principles of equality as enshrined in the Constitution. Facts of the case however, bring to focus her unequal and helpless status in an average matrimonial home. Against the husband's charges of her being "abusive, short-tempered, frigid and freak and compelling him to separate from his aged father and that her parents wanted to live on her"[28] the wife produced 11 letters of the husband, tenor of which is self-explanatory and not very uncommon. The husband wrote to her "you are not the only girl in my life, at least 100 girls had come in my life and they loved me and did everything for me—your all belongings are mine, I can starve you for days and keep your earnings, I have agreed to take you on two months probationary period, if you become pregnant, obviously I get fed up with you and leave you for ever, what you bring from there I must be brought in picture and not in the dark, I have arranged two tuitions for you for Rs. 100/- each. All the money you earn or given to you from other sources, will be mine, immediately you have to give that to me."[29] It is not surprising that the wife, a headmistress put up with all such indignities from an unemployed husband because a Hindu woman is taught to tolerate and to take marriage as a sacred institution; what is surprising is that it is the husband who still presented the petition. Against his allegations, the wife averred in her defence that she was ill-treated and was not even given medicines when she was ill and in the family way, that she was deprived of her jewellery and clothes, she clarified that her husband's allegations that she had pressed him to separate from his old father, were false because his father was a farmer and lived in a village away from them. Even against the trial court's findings that "the husband had no intentions to keep the wife but wanted to get as much money from her and her parents', the first appellate court not only decreed the husband's petition but also applauded his conduct by observing, "as the age of the girl advances, the amount also increases . . . because of the circumstances he is only taking the shrew by giving various warnings." The wife's stand was ultimately vindicated by justice V.S. Deshpande's well-founded and wise observations that "location of matrimonial home is to be determined on the basis of common convenience and benefit of parties." And that any law which gives "exclusive right to the husband to decide location of matrimonial home without considering the merits of the wife's claim would be contrary to Art. 14 and unconstitutional.[30]

That restitution petition is made for spurious objectives is reflected when a husband petitions for restitution but admits in court that he is not "prepared to keep her even if she comes to reside with him" and the court is left with no choice but to hold that "location of wife's work is an important consideration . . . in selection a matrimonial home . . . neither party has a casting vote."[31]

Restitution Petition of Husband and Wife's Predicament

A prayer for restitution is overtly a prayer for resumption of conjugal relations, but the relief is capable of manipulation and to be used for the covert and sinister object of getting rid of the spouse, divorce against whom is not otherwise possible under the existing legal grounds. It is important to note that when a petition under S. 9 is presented, the judicial focus is directed towards resotration of conjugal relations to the petitioner and consequently, when the court dissects and diagnoses the facts, efforts to restore the conjugal relations, a socially laudable objective, weigh heavily in its conscious and subconscious reasonings. Prescription resultingly is, grant of the decree which the court might not have granted, had the prayer been for divorce and not for restoration of conjugal rights. This misdirection to judicial reasoning produces results, not intended by the legislature which had allowed granting of divorce mainly due to the fault of the non-petitioner spouse. Restitution petition by a spouse, not desiring to seek restoration of conjugal relations but merely the decree, which can serve as a spring board for divorce, reveal not only his insincerity but imply the plight of the non-petitioning spouse, invariably the wife. An examination of restitution petitions shows the dilemma of the wife who was compelled to seek refuge at her parental home because of the hostile circumstances at her matrimoninal home. A restitution decree opens the doors for divorce and return to the matrimonial home means submission to her fate. S. Acharya, J., very ably unearthed in *Pramilabala's*[32] case that husband's designs for obtaining the restitution decree were "to satisfy the wishes" of his parents, so that his wife could render household services in her parents-in-law's house and he was not "particular about leading a matrimonial life with his wife." The learned judge formed this impression from the husband's failure to arrange a suitable accommodation where he and his wife could have stayed together at least for sometime in any of the places where he was posted." The learned judge was able to sift from the testimony that the husband had never bothered about his wife's "cares, anxieties and distressful condition in her father-in-law's house,"[33] caused because of his "mother's torturesome behaviour towards her" and which can be evidenced from the "stiff and stern" "tone" of his letters "bearing an imprint of his defiance and arrogance" which "indicate his insolent attitude towards his wife." The court, therefore, observed that the "wife is not a slave or an inferior member of the family" to be "compelled to stay in her parent-in-law's house against her wishes under adverse circumstances." The court found these considerations, relevant in "repelling and resisting" the relief of restitution which cannot be asked with the spirit of a despot or of a commander, for the said right is a "conjugal rights" to be enjoyed only under "congenial conditions and circumstances."[34] Similarly in *Jogindra Kaur* v. *Shivcharana Singh*,[35] the court dismissed restitution petition of the husband because he insisted his wife to go and live with his parents and declined her offer of conjugal company made inside and outside the court.

The court rightfully rejected husband's restitution petition and declared his act of keeping the wife in "illegal confinements", as "cruel" and "bound to have harmful and injurious effect on the health of the wife."[36] Similarly, Bijayesh Mukherji, J. endorsed wife's defence of reasonable excuse because her husband used to call her, a "prostitute, a whore, a fallen woman" and he had questioned in a "shameful and shameless manner the paternity of his own child, he threatened to give away the child to somebody else, and demanded back all the ornaments and presents including iron bangles" which the court righfully observed "a Hindu woman with her husband living cannot go without."[37] These findings compelled the learned Judge to turn down the husband's spurious petition for restitution.

The trend in restitution petitions unfolds that only when a wife is no longer able to put up with unbearable circumstances at the matrimonial home, that she tries to find a refuge at her native abode. Such facts make one infer that the moving force behind restitution petitions obviously cannot be the sudden desire of the husband to seek his wife's conjugal company but that re-stitution petitions were inspired by ulterior motives. However, the success of a husband in obtaining decree depends upon judicial response to social realities. So while a sensitive court may refuse the decree to a bigamous husband,[38] a callous court unmindful either of first wife's fate or of natural human emotions and impulses of self-respect in such situations, may "find no legal ground to refuse restitution to the husband."[39] In *Laxmi*

Sahuani v. *Maheshawar Sahu*[40] Restitution decree helped the husband to obtain divorce inspite of his matrimonial offence of bigamy. Cases discern wife's helpless state when she has no options but to keep living with the husband whose beatings even fracture her wrist and the husband still not able to make her leave, physically expels her and later presents a petition for restitution also. The court, trained under the norms of patriarchal and feudal culture holds "living together" as "condonation of cruelty"[41] by the battered wife.

Prejudices against a wife is so strong that a husband is palmed with the restitution decree inspite of the fact that he had himself expelled his wife after having battered her. Needless to reiterate that the effect of such decrees, and the interpretation of legal rules on such lines, helps perpetuate for a wife, similarly circumscribed, social and legal conditions which are inequitable and palsy.

The assertion that generally a husband resorts to restitution petition because it paves the way for an eventual divorce, where none can be obtained otherwise, can be amply demonstrated through reported cases. Restitution petitions defended by wives are replete with stories of the unbearable circumstances which justify their withdrawal as a "reasonable cause," but in spite of their legitimate defence, they find themselves entraped in the legal mechanism which hits them hard with the divorce decree. Such an operation of the matrimonial laws is baffling to their notions of social justice and fair play. She does not desire to live with the husband because of his cruelties nor does she wish to be divorced. His cruelties or indifference *compel her to take temporary refuge at her parent's place,* where she lives hopefully for a change of heart or change of circumstances, but instead she is forced to accept the *fait accompali* of being a divorcee. In *Rameshwari* v. *Kirpashankar*[42] the wife defended that her withdrawal was because of her husband's gambling and drinking followed by physical violence. In spite of these circumstances he was bestowed with the desired restitution decree which was later followed by a request for divorce. Lodha J., agreed to wife's submission that "proceedings under S. 9 are not to be resorted to as a device for obtaining a divorce from a wife against whom it may not be possible to prove any of the charges justifying a divorce. "A request for restitution of conjugal rights,"[43] the court observed, "should not be merely a pretence and sham and proceedings intended only with a view to obtain divorce,"[44] but nevertheless the court did award divorce. Judicial reasonings are often divorced from the orders passed by way of judgements. An in-depth analysis of cases only could have revealed judicial bias against the fair sex. It is judicial reasonings which are invariably relied upon for research and critical comments. Needless to say that it would have been impossible to fathom the wide gulf between practice and precept, between what the judge says and what he actually does. Present case is a typical example, alas! not the only one, of gender justice, while the wife had to be content with soothing and sympathetic phraseology, judgement was reserved only for the husband.

Another court lectured a wife that "tolerance was an essential virtue,"[45] when she defended husband's restitution petition alleging that he used to get drunk and beat her. Her contentions that he forced her to eat meat take drinks and that he had threatened that he would marry another woman, had also written letters to that effect to her father and other relations were summarily ignored while passing a restitution decree. Happily enough on appeal, Rajasthan High Court cogently observed that "the mutual obligations of the spouses will have to be ascertained from the statute" and that "what Manu said and his commentators wisely observed are matters only of historical interest. The court emphasized that in the present day society, a wife is "entitled to a dignified behaviour" from her husband and that the "divine status of the husband has disappeared". The court rightly held that "obstinate insistence that wife must eat meat and drink wine and threat of another marriage cumulatively constitute cruelty both physical and mental."[46]

It is unfortunate that in disregard to the legislative mandate requiring the court to "decree restitution of conjugal rights" only "on being satisfied of the truth of the statement," the decree is passed without such "satisfaction" or even husband's sincerity of keeping his wife. Though the trial court had rightly rejected husband's restitution prayer in *Sukram* v. *Mishri Bai*,[49] the High Court failed to fathom wife's predicament in the matrimonial home. Narrating the reasons for her departure from the matrimonial home, she alleged that husband's father had an evil eye on her and that instead of assuring her of his protection the husband gave her beatings and deprived her of food and clothes. It is unfortunate that the court while decreeing husband's restitution petition disregarded wife's very serious contentions. Wife's versions that she had stayed with the husband from time to time was arbitrarily picked up by the court to hold that the same had the effect of "condoning" his cruelty and the defect of child marriage was also removed by such stay. Her contentions of cruelty were ignored by the court without assigning any reasons. The facts of *N.B. Rukmini* v. *P.N. Srinivasa,*[47] represent wife's dilemma. The wife fed up with husband's ill-treatment, took shelter at the husband's sister's place and later obtained a job. While her departure was branded as 'desertion' her action of taking a few sarees led the court to conclude her intention to permanently put an end to cohabitation.'[48] Perhaps a wife has no rights even to her personal apparel even if she be without resources and be dependent. It seems that she is expected to buy, borrow or steal, for it is husband's privilege to usurp her stridhan.

The success of a shoddy restitution petition depends not upon husband's sincerity of seeking restoration of conjugal relations as S. 9 of the HMA requries, but much upon judicial conscience. For example, the Punjab High Court[50] *suo motu* took up the objection of unreasonable delay of seven years and eight months, so as to reject husband's restitution petition. The factors which carried weight with the court were, that the wife had to leave with her daughter, because she used to be battered, and also husband's neglect in providing maintenance to his wife and daughter, who the court observed "is 15 years now and of marriageable age." Though one may compliment court's comprehension of social values and attitudes, one is compelled to despise and condemn the legislative failure either in devising any effective law or any legal machinery to secure and enforce economic interests of the wife and children of the marriage. Whatever economic rights by way of maintenance are designed under the present laws, those are saddled with innumerable legal conditions[51] and when her right of maintenance is not eliminated under the tenuous and subtle legal requirements, the same is allowed to be stiffled through the presentation of a restitution petition.

Maintenance orders followed by Restitution Petitions

The clear cut pattern of a maintenance prayer or a maintenance order in favour of wife, being followed by husband's restitution petition, speaks volumes about his nefarions designs. If his petition is accepted, he succeeds not only in being able to make wife's legal rights defunct by getting the maintenance order set-aside, but it also paves the way for divorce as a perquisite.

That the request for restitution decree was not with the object of resuming cohabitation but for avoiding maintenance order in favour of wife is amply illustrated from the facts of *Kamla Bai* v. *Rathnavelu Mudaliar*.[52] The wife was compelled to find refuge at her parent's house, but as soon as she applied for maintenance the husband too presented his restitution petition. Keeping the order of maintenance in abeyance the court granted husband's prayer with the directives to put his wife in a separate portion of his house free from the domination and authority of his mother, the wife being allowed "to cook for herself and himself." The wife who went to live with her husband with hopes of finding a place in the heart of her lord and master, could not find a place of dignity even in his house. The husband had put her in a room which had no doors, and of course he never gave her his conjugal company. Wife's mother was refused the permission even to meet her daughter. Unable to tolerate any longer the life of utter isolation in an atmosphere unfit for human habitation the wife desired to go back to her parents after 19 days of thus living. The husband allowed her this grace by "taking from her the letter stating that she did not like to live with her husband and was going out of her own free will."[53] Since the attempt to prop up the marriage had miserably failed, the wife was again obliged to come to the court for maintenance; the husband contested upto the High Court on the faith of restitution decree in his favour, but the Madras High Court this time found justification in wife's living separately from her husband, and reinstated the maintenance decree of Rs. 45 per month passed by the trial court. The facts of *Jinarathanammal* v. *Srinivasa*[54] repeat the same story. In this case, wife's petition for maintenance on ground of husband's cruelty was compromised. But husband's subsequent conduct belied his intentions of being fair to his wife. The wife was obliged to apply afresh for maintenance. To counter this, he presented restitution petition. The Madras High Court however, clearly saw through his designs and while rejecting his petition gave the finding that his application was not "bona fide." It is pertinent to note that wife's socio-economic conditions drive her to sincerely make her place in the matrimonial home. Her departure from there is only in the extremely adverse circumstances. Nine years after the marriage, the wife had to leave her matrimonial home alongwith her three daughters.[55] She returned due to persuasions from elders but was kicked and thrown out. These facts obliged the court to hold that the husband was himself guilty of desertion. Rejecting his petition for restitution the court held that it was made only to "counterblast" wife's maintenance application. The Punjab case of *Tara Chand* v. *Narain Devi*[56] presents even a sadder tale. Suspecting wife's fidelity, the husband procured search warrants and went to her house accompained by police. At the time she was taken into custody her grandmother was lying dead. Her application for maintenance under S. 125 of the Criminal Procedure Code, 1973 was followed by husband's restitution petition. Surprisingly, the court relied upon husband's fancy allegations that the wife was beating him with a danda and was poisoning him. However the High Court declined to be misled and set aside the decree.

Husband's ulterior motive in procuring a restitution decree was reflected in the case of *Gur Charan* v. *Waryam Kaur*.[57] The husband had ignored his wife and child for three years and attributed immorality to the wife and had even doubted the paternity of his child. But as soon as the wife instituted proceedings for maintenance under section 488 of the Criminal Procedure Code, 1898 he presented a restitution petition. Unfortunately the court allowed the husband to manoeuvre the law and avoid his maintenance obligations towards his wife and the child. Commenting on the case, Derrett wrote, "husband's whole behaviour showed want of interest in wife or her child."[58] Setting aside the restitution decree, Honourable Justice I.D. Dua, observed, "the modern tendeny of the society is to treat with disapproval acts of violence or assault towards women."[59] The court rightly observed that "New rules of social behaviour and conduct" must find recognition with the courts while "determining what amounts to cruelty." More so, "if the victim of such assaults resents and takes exception to them."[60] In *Teja Singh* v.

Sarjit Kaur[61] the court observed that the "only intention of the appellant appeared to be to somehow or other escape the liability imposed upon him under S.488 of Cr.P.C." Facts reveal that only after the wife had obtained maintenance order under S.488 of the Cr.P.C. 1898 that the husband applied for restitution. The wife had left the husband six to seven years before because of his neglect. Rejecting his petition, Justice J.S. Bedi observed, that the "wife had a reasonable ground to suspect that her husband was carrying on with his sister-in-law with whom he was living."[62] Accounting such incidents Derrett observes that "it is a very common thing for a wife to run away (not so much from her husband, who may be inert or stupid, as from her mother-in-law), and to resort to maintenacnce proceedings under the Criminal Procedure Code." Commenting on husband's "sincere" desire, Derrett observes that "the magistrate may then be on the point of hearing her and awarding maintenance to her and her children when the husband commences proceedings for restitution and applies to the migistrate for stay of proceedings before him. . . ."[63]

The facts of these cases clearly bring out that this legal provision can be and is actually manipulated for the purpose of denying a wife even the subsistence allowance, which a court might pass in her favour through maintenance order. Grant of the decree in favour of the husband thus helps perpetuate social, economic and legal injustice, because though the role performance requires wife's complete dependance on the husband, who is also legally bound to provide her with maintenance, a restitution decree passed in his favour disentitles her to the same. *Tarak Nath Dhar* v. *Sneh Rani Dhar*[64] explains the abovesaid assertion. The facts reported are that the wife applied for maintenance under S.488 of the Cr.P.C. 1898. Her assertions that she was ill-treated by her husband and other members of the family were contested. The Court directed the husband to pay to the wife Rs. 20 per month by way of maintenance and observed that the wife had "sufficient reason for refusing to live with the husband." Instead of paying the wife any maintenance, he applied for restitution of conjugal rights. In defence, she alleged husband's cruelty. During the hotly contested case, the wife had to make several visits to the court. That the functioning of legal system is anachronistic to justice would be apparent from the fact the restitution decree cancelling previous maintenance order was passed the day the wife failed to make an appearance. The trend of decisions clearly shows that this legal remedy helps the husband to avoid his legal obligation of maintaining his wife and dependant children.

To allow use of restitution petitions for frustrating the implementation of economic obligations envisaged by law and social system is against all canons of legal and social propriety. Luckily enough, vigilant courts have been able to see through husband's inequitable designs in a large number of cases and have also checked abuse of the legal processes. However, in view of the stream of cases that are instituted for this remedy, it will be too optimistic and unrealistic to expect that this abuse would be checked in all the cases. Moreover, a restitution petition puts a halt to the obligations of payment at least during the time the petition is being processed and judicial delays are facts of common knowledge. Thus, even though a court may ultimately be able to check misuse of this legal remedy, it leaves the dependant spouse - the wife, high and dry and without any means of subsistence during the long period of litigation.

Restitution Petition by Wife

A resort to restitution petition by a wife who inspite of being rejected and abandoned by her husband and with whom she knows that only an utterly miserable and wretched life can be possible, depicts her dilemma. In a petition for divorce she forsees her social ostracization, snide and insinuating remarks and allegations on her character, lonely youth coupled with economic penury and destitution of herself and her children. Restitution petition on the other hand gives her a false hope that once the court pronounces the decree in her favour the husband will be made to obey it and she will regain an entry and acceptance in the matrimonial fold. A perusal of some of the restitution petitions presented by the wife not only give an insight into her helpless state, but also about her sincere although false hope that this legal process will somehow help her get the consortium of her husband. The facts of *Rameshchandra* v. *Premlata*[65] bring home not only the pitiable condition in which the wife is compelled to leave the husband but also that she presents the petition under an illusion of regaining entry in the matrimonial home. While doing so, she is aware that she has to submit to the husband who had inflicted cruelty upon her and, who may do so in future also. The husband and his mother had prohibited the wife from meeting any one from her parental home and cruelty of the in laws compelled her father to take the ill-conceived step of obtaining a search warrant against the husband. Later wife's father placed his cap at the husband's feet to seek his forgiveness and the wife made endless efforts so as to seek forgiveness, but the husband remained relentless. Though the court rightly found justification in wife's withdrawal and passed restitution decree in her favour one doubts whether the decree is capable of resurrecting the wife in her matrimonial home. Facts of *Jeewanti* v. *Kishan Chandra Pandey*[66] are typical example of wife's false hope of getting back her husband's conjugal company which invariably prompts her to move the court for a restitution decree. The spouses had physical intimacy prior to marriage and the wife was seven months pregnant by the husband at that time. Three days after their marriage the husband filed an annulment petition at Amorah, his native place, where neither was the marriage solemnised, nor did the parties live any time after the marriage. However, the husband was able to obtain annulment decree from Amorah. The Supreme Court, however, granted wife's prayer for restitution by giving a "broader" meaning to the term matrimonial home. The court took a realistic approach and ruled out the charges of pre-marital immorality levelled by the husband against his wife. Undoubtedly, the Supreme Court fixed the responsiblity on the husband and attempted to discourage the tendency of a man who wants to blame his wife for his own pre-marital relations with her. However, the practical effects of a restitution decree, obtained with the hope of conjugal relations by a wife are now just the opposite. Justice D.R. Khanna of the Delhi High Court[67] laments that the wife's very vital interests in the maintenance of her marriage have seriously been eroded and negated through this device. He warns the wife not to be trapped in this pretentious device, by recourse to which she has to be "ready to face the consequences of divorce."[68]

Restitution Decree and Divorce Prior to 1964 Amendment

S.13(1)(ix)[69] permitted the decree holder to make a petition for divorce if for two years after passing of the decree, it remained unsatisfied. The wife by obtaining this decree had the legal ability to make a recalcitrant husband either to accept her or else, to face the consequences of a dead-lock, because S.13(1)(ix) entitled only the "decree-holder" and not the judgment debtor, to make a petition for divorce. The husband too by obtaining this decree and in the process establishing wife's "fault," could eventually pave his way for divorce, by ensuring that the decree remained unsatisfied. However, if the husband through his actions, revealed that his motives for obtaining restitution were not sincere, the court could very well bring in S.13(1) and frustrate his designs by refusing divorce to him. Chief Justice Falshaw of the Punjab High Court rejected husband's divorce application under S.23(1) because soon after getting the decree he had instituted nullity proceedings. The court held that "it was impossible for the wife to comply with the decree for restitution as long as the husband was proceeding with the petition for nullity of the marriage."[70]

However, if a husband exercised patience for the requisite period after obtaining the decree he could then get divorce,[71] because "the compliance has to be by the judgement debtor" and a wife who did not attempt compliance of the decree, may be due to her apprehensions of cruelty or other adverse circumstances at the matrimonial home, had to face the *fait accompli* of being a divorcee.

Since the court has allowed crafty spouses to manipulate the law for their sinister designs, they have earned for themselves the charge of being "willing or co-operative ally"[72] of the willy decree-holder who could "sit cooly without making the slightest effort to follow it up." It will not be wrong to allege that as interpreter of laws, our courts have miserably failed to reject a prayer for restitution where a spouse failed to show from his conduct "sincerity," a requirement to be observed by the courts before passing a decree for restitution. Failure of judicial concern either for upholding the law or maintaining social norms is regretable.

"(F)erment of public opinion"[73] in England for the reform of their divorce laws probably inspired and influenced our legislature to introduce the principle of breakdown of marriage in the fabric of Hindu Marriage Act. It seems that while doing so, the fact that the system copied subscribes to entirely different cultural values was ignored. The 1964 amendment of HMA was enacted not only in the absence of any public opinion desiring such a change but also without any socio-legal study reflecting the desirability of such a drastic change.

It may be noted that prior to the 1964 amendment, only the decree-holder had the competenc to make a petition for divorce alleging non-resumption of cohabitation following restitution decree or else, he could create a stalemate by declining to resume cohabitation. The 1964 amendment has removed judgement debtor's disability in making a petition for divorce. The latent propensity of restitution decree being misused as an instrument to get divorce had become evident even in 1964, but unfortunately, instead of plugging this loophole, our legislature bestowed additional opportunities for divorce, and thereby initiated an unhealthy trend, probably under the belief that divorce was good for the health of Hindu society. A spouse now can commit matrimonial offence with impunity because the law allows him to get divorce irrespective of his misconduct.

Helpless state of a wife who invariably strives to retain her marital status becomes evident when one examines reported cases which unfold wife's desperate attempts towards satisfaction of restitution being frustrated by a husband bent upon obtaining a divorce. Indeed, Justice Tek Chand in the much cited case of *Syal* v. *Syal*[74] in no uncertain words evinced that the essence of a restitution decree was "that the husband desiring the company of the wife makes an effort through the court for its assistance in order to restore his wife back to him"[75] but the court instead found from the facts that "it is the wife who all along wanted to live with her husband and who was beaten when she went to live with him." The court observed "proceedings under sec. 9 were resorted to as a device . . . to obtain a divorce from a wife against whom the charges justifying a divorce could not be levelled and who was free from blame and blemish and was physically and mentally sound."[76] The court also found that the restitution proceedings were *ex-parte* and wife's contentions that she was not served with the process were neither refuted by the husband, nor was she cross-examined about these charges. The husband rather maintained a calculated silence after obtaining the decree. Rejecting his application the court observed that "the decree was intended as a step towards getting divorce" and the husband could not be allowed to take 'advantage of his own wrong.'[77]

Someswara v. *Leelavathi*,[78] also depicts wife's sincere efforts to maintain her marital status, though she had taken refuge at her parental home only in the extreme circumstances when she was no longer able to tolerate further persecution and indignity at the matrimonial home. Ignoring her difficulties or inhuman treatment, it is she who made sincerest efforts to comply, with the decree. Rejecting husband's divorce petition, the court correctly held that S. 23(1) debarred him from taking advantage of his own wrong. The court very ably prevented misuse of the decree by recording its satisfaction because it was the husband who was obstructing wife's restitution efforts for getting a divorce. Justice I.D. Dua[79] suggested that a judge had the responsibility to safeguard that the decree is not made a tool for malafide ends. In *Laxmibai* v. *Laxmichand*[80] as well the court responded to its socio-legal responsibilities. Honourable Chandrachud J. (as he then was) succinctly held that "in a petition filed under S. 13(1)(a) not only is it open to the court to consider whether the provisions mentioned in sub-sec. (1) of S. 23 are satisfied," he reminded that "the court is under an obligation to consider that question." Duly exercising its "obligation," the court held that sub-section(1) of S.23 is an "over-riding provision" and governs "any proceedings under the Act." The husband who had deliberately made no efforts to comply with the decree, found his divorce petition rejected.

Breakdown of Marriage and Section 23(1)(A)

Unfortunately, the Full Bench decision of the Delhi High Court in *Ram Kali* v. *Gopal Dass*,[81] failed to appreciate and fathom the misuse to which this remedy was put to and gave the lead of judgements which were too legalistic and yet were contrary to both statutory law as well as socio-cultural norms. The court did not bother to give a hearing to wife's prayer and contentions that a defaulting husband could not be granted divorce under the law. Unfortunately wife's legitimate objections were shelved. Court's observations that "To non-suit such a petitioner by invoking cl.(a) of sub-sec.(1) of Sec. 23 would have the effect of defeating the manifest purpose of the amending Act and reducing it to futility are regretted. Non-resumption of cohabitation after the decree of restitution leads the court to reach the conclusion that "the relations between the parties have reached a stage where there is no possibility of reconciliation." It is lamentable that this judicial legislation was followed with approval in *Madhukar Bhaskar* v *Saral Madhukar*,[82] Nain J., observed that the "enactment of Sec.13(1A) in 1964 is a legislative recognition of the principle that in the interest of society if there has been a breakdown of marriage there is no purpose in keepiong the parties tied down to each other." The learned Judge upheld the reasoning of *Ram Kali* and emphasized that "Sec.13(1A) refers to existing state of affairs" and not to the fact of "matrimonial offence or wrong." According to him this provision "provides for maintenance of true balance between respect for the binding sanctity of marriage and the social considerations which make it contrary to public policy to insist on the maintenance of a union which has utterly broken down." The Supreme Court sealed with approval the current trend of judicial interpretation in *Dharmendra Kumar* v. *Usha Kumar*[83] and observed that in order to be a "wrong" within the meaning of S.23(1)(a), "the conduct alleged has to be something more than a mere disinclination to agree to an offer of reunion", according to the court only "misconduct serious enough" can justify denial of the relief.

Thus the court, though upholds that "A request for restitution . . . should not be merely a pretence and sham" and forcefully reasons that "proceedings under S. 9 of the Act are not to be resorted to as a device for obtaining a divorce from a wife against whom it may not be possible to prove any of the charges justifying a divorce,"[84] yet divorce is granted to the husband once he succeeds in getting a restitution decree. The stigma of being a "divorcee," economic dependency, bleak chances of re-marriage amongst other reasons force a wife to seek acceptance from the husband inspite of his physical violence on her person, his heavy drinking and gambling. Husband's superior social status, economic independence and opportunity to have another bride with dowry on the other hand provide him the golden opportunity to "decline" wife's offer of conjugal relations. It may be noted that husband's firm refusal to wife's offer of conjugal relations, for which he had infact litigated, was approved by Justice Jodha without showing any concern for the wife or the impact of such interpretations on the stability of marriage as an institution of vital social interest and concern. It was held that husband's unwillingness to take back his wife "after he had applied for divorce was not a relevant consideration."[85] A perusal of these judgements leads to the singular impression that the provision of restitution of conjugal rights has lost its prime objective and instead it is being used not for bringing the warring spouses together but for permanently separating them. Marriage counselling perhaps would have helped some couples patch up their differences and resume conjugal relations. Litigation for restitution of conjugal rights however leads to poisoned relations and permanent separation of the spouses. One may find some consolation in the fact that though these judgements negated the legislative object, yet they were jurisprudentially rich and had given academically well-reasoned interpretations. However, these were followed by sheer mechanical interpretations which gave to the concept of restitution altogether a contrary meaning and colour. Justice Nathwani's observations in *Jethabhai* v. *Manabhai*[86] that "the only effect of a decree for restitution of conjugal rights is to fix the blame on the party primarily responsible for the breakdown of marriage,[87] regretably reveal lack of concern in the institution of marriage and judicial irresponsibility." In this context, the observations of M.M. Punchhi J. (as he then was) in *Jaswinder Kaur* v. *Kulwant Singh*[88] are a poor reflection of lack of awareness of the social system. The husband who had declined to yield to compassion either for the wife or for the daughter, strangely found approval for his misconduct. The court observed that an uncomplied restitution decree "gave a lever to the husband to move for divorce. Wife and daughter's pleas for compassion from the husband and prayer for court's endeavour of reconciliation were met with sarcasm. The court observed, "the time clock had started and the warning had been sounded."[89] On the expiry of time, the court remarked, "either party has been given the right to seek dissolution of marriage."[90] If that be so, one may question the need and propriety to have either the legal system or establishment of courts.

That the trend of interpreting S.13(1)(ii) has been carried rather too far will also be evident from the facts of *Santosh Kumari* v. *Mohan Lal*.[91] After obtaining the restitution decree, wife made anxious attempts to satisfy the decree. Realizing the fate of a divorcee and social ostracization following dissolution of a marriage, the wife placed her ego and individual dignity on the shelf and presented an application for execution of the decree. Undoubtedly, the nature of the decree begets execution, but its availability creates a mirage and makes financially dependent wife to incur wasteful expenses, adding to her insult and agony. Dismissing wife's application for execution the court held that "refusal to resume cohabitation inspite of execution application"[92] does not disentitle the husband from getting a divorce because an execution application fails to fulfil the requirement of compliance of the restitution decree.

Undoubtedly, a husband bent upon divorcing his wife can do so through fair or foul means. The husband in *Kamalbai* v. *Ramdas*[93] alleged that wife was of unsound mind and filed a petition for divorce in 1964. The petition was withdrawn. Few years thereafter he instead filed a petition for restitution. Spouses resumed cohabitation following a compromise between them. Ultimately, the allegation of wife being of 'unsound mind' earned him the much sought after divorce decree. It is highly improbable for a husband to withdraw a divorce petition if his wife was really of unsound mind. Since a restitution petition enables him to get a divorce through this circuitous path, it is not surprising that a husband intending to obtain divorce files a petition not for divorce but for restitution.

Recognising decree-holders' capability to create a stalemate by neither applying for divorce nor resuming cohabitation the legislature deleted S.13(ix) and inserted instead S.13(IA). Through this amendment the legislature has enabled the judgement debtor as well, to make a petition for divorce if the restitution decree remains unsatisfied for the prescribed period.[94] However, the complexity created by the 1964 amendment of the HMA. has been ably cleared by the socially and legally relevant observations of Honourable V.S. Deshpande. According to him, after the 1964 amendment both the judgement debtor as well as the decree holder are placed on the same footing as far as making of the application is concerned. Therefore, an enquiry into the conduct of the judgement debtor prior to the passing of the decree is dispensed with. But equation of judgement debtor and the decree-holder would require after the restitution decree an enquiry under S.23, into the conduct, not only of the judgement debtor but of the decree-holder also. Because as Justice Deshpande observed, "the nature of the jurisdiction of a divorce Court is not merely to decide a dispute between the parties but also to investigate not only the "facts in Court" but most importantly "facts of life." The learned justice, observed that this is because under S.23(1) "the Court has to satisfy itself that the petitioner is not in any way taking advantage of his or her own wrong or disabilty for the purpose of such relief" and that the petitioner is not guilty of various other things which may also operate as a bar to the relief. "This is also the reason," "opines the distinguished judge why under sub-section (2) of S.23, the court has to try to bring about reconciliation between the parties." Thus, by enabling the judgement debtor also to make a petition for divorce, under S.13(1A)(ii) the legislature has recognised to a "limited extent the breakdown of marriage principle." Thus S.13(1) enumerates fault grounds and S.13(1A), the breakdown of marriage concept to a limited extent. Justice Deshpande asserted that "these provisions merely enable applications for divorce to be made" on any of the grounds mentioned in S.13(1) or S.13(1A). He pointed that nowhere does the 1964 amendment suggest that "the court shall grant divorce on an application" made under S.13(1A).[95]

The learned Judge observed that "Neither sub-section (1) nor sub-section (1A) of Sec.13 is a complete code in itself for the grant of divorce." The other provisions of the Act are to be read along with them. There is no doubt that S.23A is of a general nature as it opens with the words "in any proceeding under the Act." It, therefore, applies to every proceeding under the Act. Thus, construed, the courts are bound to take into consideration conduct of the parties after obtaining the restitution decree, because the 1964 amendment merely grants to the judgement debtor of an unexecuted restitution decree a ground to apply for divorce, which he did not earlier have. The 1964 amendment, it is submitted, does not dispense with matrimonial court's duty to satisfy itself whether or not the petitioner is taking advantage of his or her own wrong. The judiciary, it is submitted, has given a much wider meaning to the 1964 amendment, not warranted by the principles of sound interpretation. The existence of S.23, which has not been deleted either by the 1964 amendment or the sweeping amendments of 1976, makes it obligatory on the court to satisfy that the petitioner is not taking advantage of his or her own wrong before granting a divorce.

Effect of 1964 Amendment

The underlying philosophy of Hindu Marriage Act, 1955, as it originally stood, was that divorce in the guise of restitution was not to be granted. Section 13(1)(ix) then in operation,[96] enabled only the decree-holder to apply for divorce. A spouse found guilty of disruption of conjugal relations could not get the restitution decree.

Before the 1964 amendment, restitution was the only matrimonial remedy to which a wife, abandoned by her husband or when made to leave him because of the unbearable circumstances at his place, could safely resort to. By making a petition for restitution, not only could she obviate the danger of an adverse legal action for divorce by the husband at a far off jurisdiction, but she could also entertain the hope of getting maintenance at least during the period of litigation. Besides, the resort to restitution petition had the effect of frustrating her husband's designs and moves towards dissolution of a marriage.

Restitution decree passed in favour of a wife provided her the choice either of dissolving the marriage, which a wife in Indian conditions, generally may not be interested, or of maintaining the facade of marriage by keeping restitution decree in her bag. Since her husband's desire to resort to divorce could thus be blocked by the restitution decree in her favour, she could use this decree as a lever to seek from the husband humane and dignified conditions, and if he still remained disagreeable, she could because of the decree being in her favour, create a deadlock. And one can surmise, that this state of things might have made some parties to patch up, though in others a never-ending dead-lock causing perpetual misery to the parties could come into existence.

However, in the Indian social context, this deadlock, though of no real and factual use, did give some emotional comfort to the wife, that if her state had been rendered miserable, the husband was in no better position. This consideration however, is not a justification for retaining a law which does not allow the parties to break a dead marriage. But this explains wife's position who, as a deserted wife, is still socially acceptable but is despised as a divorcee. The only justification in retaining the pre-1964 position can be that the restitution decree then, because of the disability of the judgement debtor to petition for a divorce, was not as much susceptible to abuse, as it has become after removal of the disability. The effects of 1964 amendment, and more particularly the liberal, interpretation given by the courts adversely affect wife's interests who in a majority of cases, desires to retain her marital status. After the 1964 amendment, a wife by obtaining a restitution decree digs the grave of her own marriage, because one year (two years before the 1976 amendment) after the decree her husband can present a divorce petition. Hence, a wife desiring to maintain her marriage will be ill-advised to resort to this matrimonial remedy which presents the facade of restoring the conjugal relations but enables the opposite party obtain a divorce in situations, wherein he cannot obtain it otherwise.

Now a wife abandoned by her husband or compelled to leave him on the face of adverse circumstances, has no legal remedy short of divorce. She cannot commence any action under the HMA. for maintenance because these provisions can be resorted to only during the pendency of proceedings,[97] or after a decree or order[98] has been passed under the Act. A resort to S.125 of the Cr.P.C. for maintenance may be ill-advised since an action even if it is for getting maintenance, under the provisions of Cr.P.C. leaves an aura of 'criminal action' taken by the wife against her husband. Matrimonial courts have invariably construed such an action as an act of cruelty by the wife.[99] Moreover, this is a short term measure to be resorted to in an emergency alone. In practice too, S.125 of Cr.P.C. is not much resorted to.[100]

Matrimonial cases abundantly bring to notice the misuse to which this matrimonial remedy is susceptible and in fact, it is being exploited by the socially and economically stronger party. The liberal interpretation given to the 1964 amendment tends to ignore the moral, emotional, economic and social compulsions of a wife whose sincere attempts towards compliance of the restitution decree are thwarted by the opposite party and the same are not considered as a "wrong" within the meaning of S.23(1). The liberal interpretation though takes note of the fact of breakdown of marriage which is not a statutory ground for divorce, but ignores the fact that divorce under the Hindu Marriage Act, as a rule is granted without even fixing, let alone on a rational basis, the economic responsibility of the husband towards the divorced wife or even the children. This liberal interpretation in the existing framework of the matrimonial laws and practice is inequitable to the wife and sets a socially unhealthy trend in divorce litigation.

Plea for Deletion of Section 9

The *raison d'être* of restitution petition is restoration of conjugal rights. This implies "right to each other's society" and "marital intercourse."[101] Since the decree can be specifically enforced,[102] Justice P.A. Chaudary of the Andhra Pradesh High Court observes that enforcement of the decree can "alter irretrievably" the "life pattern of the wife."[103] Specifying that "it is the wife who has to beget and bear a child"[104] the learned judge observed that enforcement of the decree "cripples the wife's future plans of life and prevents her from using that self-destructive remedy." The court held that enforcement of the decree can "foist pregnancy against her will through state action . . . such a law violates the right to privacy and human dignity guaranteed by Art. 21 of the Constitution."[105] Since in its operation the remedy creates arbitrary and inequitable results, it is *ultra vires* of Art.14 of the Constitution. The court rightly observed that no overwhelming state interest justified "the subordination of vulnerable right to privacy to any state interests."[106] S.9 of the H.M.A. violates Art.21 of the Constitution and is void. Justice Avadh Behari Rohtagi of the Delhi High Court[107] dissented from Andhra authority because according to him "restitution aims at cohabitation and consortium," and it "does not enforce sexual intercourse.[108] It may be submitted that a wife compelled to join the matrimonial home may have to subject herself to sexual intercourse against her will, because of her physical weakness.

Besides forcible sexual intercourse, a revengeful husband may malign her further by charging her of unchastity after having made her submit to him through force. However, these problems may be considered rather academic in view of the general practice of restitution decree being used solely as a "stepping stone to divorce."[109] Since the decree, as the matrimonial cases show, fails to fulfil its avowed object of restoring conjugal rights between the spouses, and it is used for the sinister object of obtaining divorce on a ground not afforded by the legislature, there is no reason to keep it in the statute book. As the remedy is "uncivilized," the British Parliament through section 20 of the Matrimonial Proceedings and Property Act, 1970 abolished the right to claim this remedy.[110] Since "there are no overwhelming state interests" justifying sacrifice of "individual's precious constitutional right to privacy"[111] there are arguments that the provision be abolished.[112]

Conclusion

The law and practice concerning restitution has revealed that neither our legislature nor our judiciary is concerned about the effect of this legal provision[113] on the vital and cardinal interests of a Hindu wife in the maintenance of her marital status and that of the society's to have stable marriages. Rather, it emerges from the studies that legislative as well as judicial efforts have consistently been to maintain and promote patriarchal and feudal set-up wherein the wife should submit herself without complaint to each and every wrong inflicted on her by her husband and his family members, a complaint and resentment against which exposes her to the danger of being rejected, thrown out and divorced.

It may be reiterated that S.9 of the HMA, before it was amended in 1964, had remarkabley revealed its penchant in aiding a wife to maintain her marital status. Monogamous[114] nature of the Hindu Marriage had thwarted husband's patriarchal right of disowning the wife who resented his authority and of remarrying. The legislature[115] therefore within merely 9 years of the passing of the Act and of discovering a Hindu Male's unfavourable condition under the provision, amended it. The effect has been disastrous on the interests of the Hindu wife who has been disrobed of this singular right which had aided her to demand a dignified acceptance for herself in the matrimonial home because of her capacity to create a deadlock. Since the law of monogamy had deprived a husband the liberty of remarriage without divorcing his first wife, our legislature allowed the judgement debtor, invariably a husband, to seek divorce just a year after the passing of the restitution decree and of its non-compliance. Thus, a wife's interests in the maintenance of marriage have been sacrificed at the altar of a husband's patriarchal and feudal privileges.

Judiciary still could have, had it desired to do so, salvaged the Hindu wife's social, matrimonial and constitutional rights by giving S.23(1)(a)[116] a just, logical, legally correct and socially relevant interpretation. What's amazing is that while the legislative intervention[117] was to liberalise the Hindu law of divorce in tune with the western law presuming that the Hindu society had transformed itself and had become as open, liberal and individualistic as the western society, judicial pretentions were "to preserve the marriage"[118] by granting divorce.

It has been forcefully argued that non-compliance of the restitution decree is an "indicia that the parties have reached a stage of no return",[119] however, the same is merely based on presumptions. It has not been studied through relevant case analysis whether such social attitudes have been generated by the judicial interpretations which pronounce that refusal to accept back the wife following restitution decree is not a wrong within the meaning of S.23(1)(a). Thus non-compliance of the decree may be because the husband knows that through this decree he has already earned the right to get rid of his wife. Surprisingly, the court while pretending to promote stability of marriage through this decree, advocates that (restitution) is "a passage or passport to divorce."[120] Thus, legislature as well as judiciary have sided with the husband to legalize the law of jungle that might is right. The socially and economically privileged spouse has also the legal system to back him and he can legally accept or reject the wife as if she was on probation.

It is not being argued that our judiciary almost always sides with the husband, what is definitely emerging from the case analysis is that judgements are invariably pronounced in favour of the husband. It is possible that while deciding the cases on family law, the courts ignore the ethos and culture of the family relations. One of the important factors which is lost sight of is that it is the wife who has to leave her parents to join the husband who continues to stay with his kith and kin even after the marriage. Hence it is the wife alone who has to seek acceptance for herself in the matrimonial home. A wife who humbly requests "some elderly persons in the family to take the responsibility that she would not be ill-treated in the matrimonial home"[121] is coldly told by our judge who is indifferent to her problems that "such an expectation from the husband cannot constitute a good ground"[122] to leave the matrimonial home. Instead divorce is the proper and befitting reward for her unreasonable conduct of desiring her safety in the matrimonial home.

The philosophy of our highest court is not different in this regard. Though the counsel for the wife had beseeched their Lordships of the Supreme Court to consider the reality of the Indian society where "a divorced wife would be materially at a great disadvantage."[123] The court conceding this submission as correct, directed the husband to pay Rs. 200 per month as maintenance to the wife and Rs. 300 per month for the daughter till her marriage. As if Rs. 500 per month, presuming that it is paid regularly,[124] would be a reasonable compensation both in terms of their reasonable financial requirements as also for the deprived socio-cultural status. It is an important fact that the husband had consented for the passing of restitution decree but "thereafter refused to cohabit with the wife."[125] The contention of the wife's counsel that this was to "mislead the wife and the court" was rejected. The Supreme Court sealed wife's rights by observing that restitution decree "serves a social purpose as an aid to the prevention of break up of marriages"[126] and yet pronounced divorce. The Court agreed that restitution decree was a "trap" but declared that "the marriage had broken down."[127] Thus, through contrived interpretation, judicial legislation,[128] and by ignoring the legislative mandate under S.23(1)(a) of the Act a husband's patriarchal right to reject a wife have been forged and wife's genuine rights to seek humane treatment at the matrimonial home and the right to sustain her marriage have been sacrifised.

The erosion of the Hindu wife's right has culminated to the ignoble extent of indignity and insult. An offer of Rs. 2 per month as maintenance by a bigamous husband to the wife in a restitution case smacks of humiliating insult not only to the wife in question but to the Hindu woman and institution of marriage. Thus, in spite of the sacramental and monogamous nature of the Hindu marriage, the husband after having committed bigamy, could still get the divorce because through the "consent decree"[129] the wife ought to have joined him though "he had no obligation to take the plaintiff back to his house."[130] The court while agreeing that according to customs prevalent amongst the Hindus, the wife is not expected to "go and report the husband's house for restitution," yet the court affirmed an order of Rs. 60 per month while rejecting her prayer of Rs. 500 as maintenance though she had argued that the husband owned 10 acres of land. The court felt that the husband was "under legal obligation to take back the plaintiff" yet she was denied even the right to sustain herself. Perhaps the judges from their ivory tower are unaware that even a wife is a human being and cannot survive on such amount. Not only the wife was wronged by the husband, she was not spared even economic injustice by the Goddess of Justice.[131] The cases reveal a calously casual approach towards the legal rights of the wife. Indeed, it might have shocked the Goddess of Justice to learn from the unambiguous declaration of Honourable A.B. Rohtagi J., "In the privacy of the home and the married life neither Art. 21 nor Art.14 have any place."[132] Paras Diwan rightly questions "should we go back to the Roman concept of patriarchal home where the writ of the State could not run beyond the threshold of the Roman Patriarch, and within the four-walls of his home he could with impunity butcher a calf, cow, slave, son, daughter or wife."

It emerges from the case analysis that wife's restitution petition is generally moved with a desire to re-enter her husband's home, cases also reveal her earnest attempts to comply with the restitution decree of the husband, which are however, thwarted by the husband who invariably desires dissolution of the marriage. Husband's restitution petition however shows altogether different motives and designs. Dissolution of a marriage works against the interests of a wife.[133] Law concerning restitution as it stands today offer a barbarous choice to the woman and that is either to suffer without protest or get divorced. In view of the facts which emerge from the reported cases, it is submitted that the interpretations of the Delhi High Court in *Ram Kali*[134] as well as *Harvinder Kaur's*[135] cases and that of the Supreme Court in *Saroj*

Rani's[136] and *Dharmendra Kumar's*[137] cases are unjust and arbitrary and need to be reviewed to uphold the constitutional[138] and legal rights of the wife. The contrived and legalistic interpretation of the section has subterfuged the content and meaning of restitution. Natural and ordinary interpretation on the other hand is not only just and proper but it also protects the legitimate interests of the wife. The Judgement of Devinder Gupta and Lokeshwar Singh Panta J.J.[139] in this respect illuminates a fresh approach. The Court gave due weightage to the wife's contention that the husband who was now making a petition for divorce alleging cruelty and desertion, had earlier made a petition for restitution. Social realities impelled the court to perform its statutory duties under S.23(1)(b). Thus, though the wife had not specifically pleaded condonation by the husband, the court held, "when a petition is filed claiming a decree of restitution, it clearly stipulates that the person seeking relief has no grouse or cause of complaint against the other spouse and even if there was any cause of complaint, the same has been condoned or forgiven. The intention being to resume cohabitation."[140] The court accepted wife's appeal and candidly observed, "it is our duty under S.23(1)(b) to find out whether cruelty was condoned by the appellant." The court reached this conclusion because the alleged acts of cruelty by the wife were committed prior to the husband's petition for restitution.[141] From his restitution petition the court inferred condonation of the alleged cruelty and thus estopped him from reviving the condoned acts of cruelty.

Thus, restitution of conjugal rights when given its natural meaning, offers a ray of hope to the wife, hope which had almost withered away. It had extinguished when restitution decree was encashed for divorce, when the spouse himself guilty of matrimonial offence could also get divorce and when a spouse thwarting the attempts for restoration of conjugal relations could still divorce on the spacious plea that there is a failure in resumption of conjugal relations. He can do so even today—the need is to review the judgements and legislation which have distorted the content and meaning of restitution beyond recognition. Law must serve the needs of the society.[142] The pre-1964 amended provision of law on restitution served to a limited extent the needs of a Hindu wife and it should be restored to its original content. The wife who alone has to leave the parental home to join that of the husband's, must have the choice to find a temporary anchor during the time of crisis. It does not serve any social purpose to foreclose her choice.[143]

NOTES AND REFERENCES

1. Hindu Marriage Act, 1955, hereinafter to be referred as HMA.
2. Section 9 of the Hindu Marriage Act, 1955.
3. *T.Sareetha* v. *T. Venkata Subbaiah*, AIR 1983 A.P. 356 at 370.
4. Restitution of Conjugal Rights.
5. *Supra* note 3.
6. *Ibid.*
7. S. 9(2) stated "Nothing shall be pleaded in answer to a petition for restitution of conjugal rights which shall not be a ground for judicial separation or nullity of marriage or for divorce." The subsection has been deleted by the 1976 amendment of the Hindu Marriage Act, 1955.
8. A.I.R. 1975 A.P. 239.
9. *Id.* at 240.
10. *Ibid.*
11. *Id.* at 241.
12. A.I.R. 1966 M.P. 212.
13. *Id.* at 214.
14. *Tirath Kaur* v. *Kirpal Singh*, A.I.R. 1964 Punj. 28.
15. *Id.* at 30.
16. *Ibid.*
17. 1977 Hindu L.R. 175, see also *Surinder* v. *Gurdeep*, A.I.R. 1973 P & H. 134.
18. Paras Diwan, 'Wife's Refusal to Give up her job and the Husband's Petition for Restitution of Conjugal Rights'. XX. *The Law Review*, 6(1968).
19. *Supra* note 14.
20. *Supra* note 8.
21. *Supra* note 12.
22. Sec. 9 of the HMA, 1955 provides "when either the husband or wife had, without reasonable excuse, withdrawn from the society of the other, the aggrieved party, may apply, by petition to the District court, for restitution of conjugal rights and the court, on being satisfied of the truth of the statement made in such petition and that there is no legal ground why the application should not be granted, may decree restitution of conjugal rights accordingly.
23. A.I.R. 1975 Mad. 331.
24. *Id.* at 332.
25. A.I.R. 1977 Raj. 113.
26. *Ibid.*
27. A.I.R. 1978 Del. 296.
28. *Id.* at 301.
29. *Ibid.*
30. *Id.* at 301.
31. *Pravinaben* v. *S.T. Arya*, A.I.R. 1975 Guj. 69.
32. *Pramilabala Barik* v. *Rabindranath Barik*, A.I.R. 1977 Ori. 132.

33. *Id.* at 134. So also in *K. Babu Rao* v. *K. Ammaji* A.I.R. 1991 (NO.C) 30 (Andh. Pra.) a case under sections 10 and 32 of the Divorce Act, 1869, the court rejected husband's restitution petition, as it was his device to get rid of wife's maintenance claim or a partition suit. The court considered husband's aspersions on wife's character and denying paternity of his two children born out of their wedlock as constituting mental cruelty to wife.
34. *Supra* note 32 at 136.
35. A.I.R. 1965, J & K. 95 (98).
36. *Gurdev Kaur* v. *Sarwan Singh*, A.I.R. 1959 Punj. 162 (at 166)
37. *Bejoy Daw* v. *Smt. Aloka Daw*, A.I.R. 1969 Cal. 477 at 430.
38. *Thenku Veeriah* v. *Tamisetti Nagiah*, A.I.R. 1959 A.P. 547 at 550. (F.B.)
39. *Mst. Premi* v. *Daya Ram*, A.I.R. 1965 H.P. 15(16).
40. A.I.R. 1985 Orissa 11.
41. *Gindan* v. *Barelal*, A.I.R. 1976 M.P. 83.
42. A.I.R. 1975 raj. 28.
43. *Id.* at 30.
44. *Ibid.*
45. *Chand Narain Gautam* v. *Saroj Gautam*, A.I.R. 1975 Raj. 88.
46. *Id.* at 92.
47. A.I.R. 1984 Karnt 131.
48. *Id.* at 134.
49. A.I.R. 1979 M.P. 144. So also the court refused to grant restitution decree at the request of the husband who alleges wife to be guilty of adultery. Though it may be otherwise improbable for a husband to desire conjugal relations with a wife whom he alleges to be guilty of adultery, but the desire to obtain divorce through the restitution decree inspires him to make a petition for it. See *O.P. Mehta* v. *Saroj Mehta* A.I.R. 1984 Delhi 159.
50. *Jasmel Singh* v. *Gurnam Kaur*, A.I.R. 1975 P. & H. 225.
51. Maintenance *under S. 24 of the Act* is available only during the litigation period. And an order for alimony can be passed only when a decree is passed. If the parties are separated and there is an absence of litigation or there had been litigation but the same is either dismissed in default or otherwise then no alimony can be granted. Moreover, a spouse guilty of matrimonial offense is not granted maintenance. Nor is maintenance ordered for a wife who was trapped in a void marriage.
52. A.I.R. 1965 Mad. 88.
53. *Ibid.*
54. A.I.R. 1964 Mad. 482.
55. A.I.R. 1981 A.P. 123.
56. A.I.R. 1975 P & H. 300.
57. A.I.R. 1960 Punj. 422.
58. J.Duncan M., Derrett, *The Death of a Marriage Law*, 153 (1978).
59. *Gurcharan* v. *Waryam Kaur*, *supra* note 57 at 425.
60. *Ibid.*
61. A.I.R. 1962 Punj. 195.
62. *Id.* at 196.
63. J. Duncan M. Derrett, *supra* note 58 at 326.
64. A.I.R. 1949 Cal. 87.
65. A.I.R. 1979 M.P. 15. So also the wife though obtained the decree of restitution,

she perhaps was not advised that the decree of restitution would pave the way for the husband to divorce her. The husband who had dumped her in her father's home would not bring her to the matrimonial home merely because the court had passed a restitution decree in her favour. *Sushila Bai* v. *Prem Narayan* A.I.R. 1986 M.P. 225.

66. A.I.R. 1982 S.C. 3.
67. *Santosh Kumari* v. *Kewal Krishan* A.I.R. 1985 Delhi 393.
68. *Id* at 395.
69. As the law originally stood prior to 1964 amendment of the HMA.
70. *Ishwar Chander Ahluwalia* v. *Smt. Promila Ahluwalia*, A.I.R. 1962 Punj. 432.
71. *Gulab Kaur* v. *Gurdev Singh Rattan*, A.I.R. 1963 Punj. 493.
72. Rajkumari Agrawala, *Matrimonial Remedies*, 22 (1974).
73. Justice V.S. Deshpande, "Divorce under the Hindu Marriage Act - A Conflict of Principles," A.I.R. 1971 (Journal) 113. Emphasis added.
74. A.I.R. 1968 P.H. 489.
75. *Id*. at 491.
76. *Id*. at 492.
77. *Id*. at 495.
78. A.I.R. 1968 Mys. 274.
79. *Shreevastava* v. *Mrs. Veena*, A.I.R. 1965 Punj. 54.
80. A.I.R. 1968 Bom.322, (1967), 70 Bom. L.R. 80.
81. I:L.R. (1971) 1 Del. 6.
82. A.I.R. 1973 Bom. 55.
83. A.I.R. 1977 S.C. 2218 at p. 2220
84. *Supra* note 42 at 30.
85. *Id*. at 32. Husband need not even make a pretence because he can have divorce just on demand. The husband filed a petition for restitution and in the alternative a petition for divorce. Wife's objections and also writ petition under Article 226 that both the reliefs prayed for were contradictory, were summarily rejected because under the provisions of Civil Procedure Code an alternate relief could be obtained. *Krishna Devi* v. *Addl. Civil Judge*, Bijnor A.I.R. 1985 All 131.
86. A.I.R. 1975 Bom. 88 at 105.
87. *Ibid*.
88. A.I.R. 1980 P & H 220.
89. *Id*. at 222.
90. *Ibid*.
91. A.I.R. 1980 P & H 325.
92. *Ibid*.
93. A.I.R. 1981 Bom. 187.
94. Which under S. 13(1A) was two years and after the 1976 amendment is one year under the substituted S. 13(1A) (ii).
95. *Supra* note 73. In this context we may note *Mita Gupta* v. *Prabir Kumar* A.I.R. 1989 Cal. 248. The court held that mere non-compliance with the RCR decree was not a wrong under S. 23(i) (a). Wife's attempts at restitution were thwarted by the husband by refusing her entry in the matrimonial home and he was granted divorce under S. 13(1A) ii of the HMA.
96. Under S. 13(i) (ix) only the decree-holder of an unsatisfied restitution decree, who had established his innocence and other party's guilt, was given the right to make a petition for divorce.

97. S. 24 of the HMA.
98. S. 25 of the HMA.
99. Court construed a complaint to husband's employer for maintenance as cruelty. *Parihar* v. *Parihar*, A.I.R. 1978 Raj. 140.
100. In the sample period of 1978, 1979 and 1980 the number of cases reported in the A.I.R. on S. 125 of the Code of Criminal Procedure, 1973 were only 5 as against 77 matrimonial cases. Devinder Kumari Raheja "Maintenance and Custody Orders: To be part of Main Proceedings," *VII Kurukshetra Law Journal*, 61 (1981).
101. *T. Sareetha supra* note 2 at 356.
102. Order 21, Rule 32 and 33 of the C.P.C. entitle the decree holder to get financial sanctions against the judgement debtor of the restitution decree. Thus respondent's property alone is subject to attachment. The Law Commission in its 57th Report did not recommend its repeal. Physical execution of RCR by way of respondent's arrest is not however possible.
103. *Supra* note 2 at 373.
104. *Ibid.*
105. *Id.* at 370.
106. *Ibid.*
107. *Harvinder kaur* v. *Harmander Singh*, A.I.R. 1984 Del. 66.
108. *Id.* at 76 para 56. Paras Diwan rightly observed, "how many people young or not very young) will accept cohabitation minus sexual intercourse. For that one has to be a Brahma Kumari. *Modern Hindu Law* at 178 (1990).
109. *Supra* note 107, at 76 para 56.
110. The British Law Commission, presided over by Mr. Justice Scarman, recommended its abolition.
111. *Supra* note 98, at 370. Infact the court in *Nitu* v. *Krishan Lal*, A.I.R. 1992 Del. 1, upheld wife's right to stay away from the husband who through legal notice had made a "pre-emptory call" preceded by such allegations which a self-respecting woman howsoever humble her parents or brothers might be would not have pocketed . Wife's refusal is justified as she should not be compelled to face life long humiliation at the hands of a husband, bereft of those delicate feelings which add meaning, and lend charm to matrimonial relations. Thus the husband could not make a case of wife's desertion.
112. Bhardwaj, Aparna, The Restitution of Conjugal Rights, A Remedy or An Evil under The Modern Hindu Law, unpublished LL.M. dissertation submitted to Kurukshetra University.
113. Though generally termed a 'remedy' it would be a misnomer to call it so. Granting dissolution to a spouse desiring and striving restitution of conjugal rights can hardly be considered a remedy.
114. Introduced by the Hindu Marriage Act, 1955.
115. *Supra* note 69. It is pertinent to note that 38 years after the passing of the Hindu Marriage Act, our Parliament still has not even entertained the idea let alone having enacted legislation concerning the wife's right to share with the husband matrimonial property accumulated and earned during the marriage. The husband alone is allowed to unjustifiably use the fruits of wife's contributions as a home maker.
116. *Supra* note 80.
117. By way of amendment of S.9 of the HMA.
118. *Harvinder Kaur* v. *Harmander Singh* A.I.R. 1984 Delhi 66 at p. 70.
119. *Id.* at p. 71.

120. *Id.* at p. 73.
121. *Bhawana Advani* v. *Manohar Advani* AIR 1992 M.P.105.
122. *Ibid.* Husband had presented a restitution petition and the wife consented the decree desiring intervention of elderly persons and this consent decree was enough for the husband to get a divorce decree.
123. *Saroj Rani* v. *Sudershan Kumar*, A.I.R. 1984 S.C. 156 at 1569.
124. The Law Commission of India in its Seventy Third Report on criminal liability for failure by husband to pay maintenance or permanent alimony granted to the wife by the court under certain circumstances recommended rigorous imprisonment of the defaulter while acknowledging "the tendency on the part of the husbands to stop payment of alimony or maintenance even though a decree or an order for this purpose has been made in favour of their wives."
125. *Supra* note 123 at 1568.
126. *Id.* at 1566.
127. *Ibid* see also *Dharmendra Kumar* v. *Usha Kumar* AIR 1977 S.C.2218.
128. Though the Law Commission in its Seventy First Report on the Hindu Marriage Act 1955, had recommended to introduce Irretrievable Breakdown of Marriage as an additional ground and though a Bill to that effect (The Marriage Laws (Amendment) Bill, 1981. Bill No. 23 of 1981, introduced in Lok Sabha on 27th February 1981) was also introduced in the Parliament, but the same has not as yet become law.
129. *Laxmi Sahuani* v. *Maheswar Sahu*, A.I.R. 1985 Orissa 11.
130. *Id.* at 14.
131. Section 18 of the Hindu Adoptions and Maintenance Act, 1956 entitles wife to have a separate residence and claim maintenance from the husband and the wife had staked her claims under this Act also.
132. *Supra* note 107 at 75.
133. Paras Diwan, *Modern Hindu Law* 1990, at 178.
133. "In the Hindu religion, woman had only one 'dharma' that is pativrata'. For a woman there is only one God, the husband." Maurya, Sahab Deen, *Women in India*, at 6 Chugh Publications (1988). The author laments, "Hindu culture has erred on the side of the excessive subordination of the wife to the husband. This has resulted in the husband sometimes usurping and exercising authority that reduces him to the level of brute." *Id.* at 1.
134. *Supra* note 81.
135. *Supra* note 107.
136. *Supra* note 123.
137. *Supra* note 83.
138. Article 14 of the Indian Constitution provides equality before law and equal protection of the laws. Section 9 of the HMA provides equality before law in as much as both husband as well as the wife may make the petition for restitution of conjugal rights. But since both the spouses are differently placed as regards the site of matrimonial home is concerned, wife's departure from there under compelled circumstances giving a licence to the husband to divorce her through the instrumentality of restitution would amount to denial of equal protection of the Laws. At present RCR imposes through court order the will of one party over the other and the same is violative of the legal rights as well as dignity and honour of the other.
139. *Nirmala Devi* v. *Ved Prakash* AIR 1993 H.P. 1.
140. *Id.* at 6.

141. *Ibid.* Wife's allegations that the father-in-law wanted to have illicit relations with her and that she had to work hard and was denied the necessary amenities made the husband to petition for divorce on ground of cruelty and desertion. Wife filed a petition under S.125 of the Cr.P.C. before the Gram Panchayat and was awarded Rs.100 per month as maintenance. The plea of desertion was later on given up. The husband had also alleged cruelty because when he was sick the wife did not come to see him. The parties were married 12-13 years back. However the husband had earlier filed a restitution petition, which the court held must have been moved with an intention to resume normal cohabitation and thus cruelty even assuming had been committed by the wife, was condoned by the husband.
142. Divorce affects children of the marriage too. Vasantha R.R.Patri quotes from Wallerstein and Blakeslee's book "second chances" that "children tend to interpret the parental divorce as a rejection of themselves. They "experience an acute powerlessness at not being able to keep the erring parents in check." Since their wishes, fears and concerns are "totally overlooked during the process of divorce," they carry "painful memories of the divorce of their parents even decades later." Though the anxiety of divorce is their legacy." surprisingly when "divorce occurs the focus is totally on the adult". The *Hindustan Times*, Feb.21, 1993. It may be pointed out that divorce under the provisions of HMA is granted without even an enquiry about the existence of the children of the marriage. Nothing is done to ensure an attempt to reassure the children that their needs and interests will be looked after, the studies rather reveal that alongwith the wife children of the marriage are also rejected and in the absence of any financial safeguards of their interests they are left to the mercies of God. Thus divorce may become instrumental in wrecking the society, especially when it is granted just at the wishes of one spouse.
143. Wife's right to maintain her marital status does not conflict with the interest of the society to have stable marriages. The pre-1964 amendment provision does not foreclose husband's option for divorce. He would be free to get dissolution on the grounds provided by the statute.

MINOR BRIDES AND MARITAL RAPE

*Kusum**

Minor Brides[1]

The last few years have witnessed a lot of debate on issues pertaining to girl child. In fact the year 1990 was observed as the year of the Girl Child in the SAARC region, with focus on various problems of female children and deliberations and discussions to solve them.

One aspect which needs serious thought and action is the problem of minor brides with all its evil consequences like early maternity, weak children, early widowhood, etc.

It may be noted that prior to the Penal Code of 1860, there was no provision prohibiting the cohabitation of a man and his wife–whatever her age. The Law Commissioners who drafted the Indian Penal Code in 1846 mooted the idea of penalising consummation of marriage below a certain age. The Code of 1860 fixed the age at 10 and the husband who consummated the marriage with his wife who was below 10 years of age was to be held guilty of rape. The punishment prescribed for the offence could extend to transportation for life.

For 30 years this continued to be the legal position. In view of several cases, however, it came to be realised that the law was not satisfactory. In this context, a reference may be made to a case from Bengal, *Queen Empress* v. *Huree Mohun Mythee*[2] (Calcutta, 1891). A fully developed adult man was charged with causing the death of his wife, a girl aged 11 years and 3 months, who had not attained puberty. The girl died of haemorrhage from rupture caused in the course of cohabitation. It was argued on behalf of the husband that no offence was committed as the wife was not under 10 years.

*Associate Research Professor, Indian Law Institute.

The Court did not accept this argument. The observations of Justice Wilson are pertinent in this context. He said:[3]

> "It by no means follows that because the law of rape does not apply as between husband and wife, if the wife has attained the age of ten years, that the law regards a wife of that age as a thing made over to be the absolute property of her husband, or as a person outside the protection of the criminal law. Under no system of law with which courts have to do in this country. . . has it ever been the law that a husband has the absolute right to enjoy the person of his wife without regard to the question of safety to her, as for instance, if the circumstances be such that it is certain death to her, or that is probably dangerous to her life."

> He continued:[4]

> "The law, it is true, is exceedingly jealous of any interference in matters marital, and very unwilling to trespass inside the chamber where husband and wife live together, and never does do except in cases of absolute necessity. But the criminal law is applicable between husband and wife wherever the facts are such as to bring the case within the terms of the penal code." Consequently, in 1891 a Bill was introduced to raise the age from 10 to 12.

The object of the Bill was "to protect female children from immature prostitution and from premature cohabitation." Awareness was beginning to grow on the evil consequences of early marriage and early consummation. Child welfare centres were set up, baby shows and child welfare exhibitions held, to focus on the evils and problems of child marriage. In 1924, Dr. Hari Singh Gour introduced a Bill to further amend the rape provision in Section 375 of the Penal Code raising the age to 14 years in both marital and extra-marital cases. The Bill was referred to the Select Committee which reduced the age from 14 to 13 in the case of marital rape.

Opinion on the Bill being sharply divided it could not get through. However, public opinion was very strong on the need to raise the age for marriage or consummation. In 1925, the age for legal consummation of marriage was raised to 13. Another Bill was introduced in 1927 to raise the age of consent in marital cases to 14, and in extra-marital cases to 16. The Age of Consent Committee was set up to consider the matter. During this period it also came to be realised that it would be better to prevent early marriages than raise the age of consummation after marriage.

Several proposals were put forward by social workers and educationists to discourage child marriages, like, excluding from the educational institutions boys below a certain age who were married, or, at any rate, to exclude such boys from sitting for particular examinations. It was, however, realised in the course of time that such measures would not be effective and the only effective or deterrent way to stop such marriages was by prohibiting them and imposing a penalty in case of contravention of the prescribed age limits.

In 1927, Rai Sahib Haribilas Sarda introduced a Bill to restrain the solemnisation of child marriages among Hindus declaring such marriages as invalid. The Bill penalised husbands over 18 marrying girls below 14. It also penalised parents, guardians and priests solemnising marriages of such boys and girls. This Bill was also referred to the Select Committee for opinion and discussion. There was a lot of opposition from various quarters. Some of the arguments of the opponents were :

(1) That it would amount to encroachment upon matters of domestic and social nature.

(2) That the government, being foreign, is neither competent nor entitled to force such a law on persons belonging to different races and religions. Any interference would amount to violation of the pledge of neutrality in matters of religion referred to in the Queen's Proclamation.

(3) That the increase in the age of consent for consummation or fixing minimum age for marriage could amount to interference with the religious laws, rights and customs of the Hindus and Muslims, e.g. among Brahmins and some other castes, post-puberty marriage is a sin and so also non-consummation of marriage within 16 days of the wife's first periods.

(4) That the morality of the boys and girls may suffer if they are not married soon after puberty.

(5) That legislation fixing the age of consummation derogates from the rights conferred upon the husband by marriage.

Despite all opposition, however, the Committee was inclined to bring reforms. It observed :

"Although it is true that the proposed legislation touches a very delicate chord regarding the most personal and intimate relations between human beings, that fact does not exempt it from interference by the legislature on a proper case being made out, either to prevent a shocking evil or to further social justice. It may be remarked that in every civilised country, legislation has been used as a remedy to remove social injustice and other evils of that character. . ."

The Committee agreed that early maternity was a great evil."It contributes very largely to maternal and infantile mortality; in many cases wrecks the physical system of the girl and generally leads to degeneracy in the physique of the race." Comparing Sati with early maternity, the Committee remarked, "Satis were few and far between. They compelled attention by the enormity of the evil in individual cases, by the intense agony of the burning widow and the terrible shock they gave to humane feelings. But after all, they were cases only of individual suffering; the agony ended with the martyr and the incident had some compensation in the martyr being almost deitified as an ideal Hindu *Pativrata*, a devoted wife, the subject of adoration after death. . . .

In the case of early maternity, however, the evil is widespread and affects such a large number of women, both amongst Hindus and Muslims, as to necessitate redress. It is so extensive as to affect the whole framework of society. After going through the ordeal, if a woman survives the age of 30, she is in many cases an old woman, almost a shadow of her former self. Her real life is a long lingering misery and she is a sacrifice at the altar of custom . . . . If legislation was justified for preventing Sati, there is ample justification for legislation to prevent early maternity, both on the grounds of humanity and in the furtherance of social justice".

Consequently reforms were made and the age for marriage and consent raised. The Sarda Bill was enacted known as the Child Marriage Restraint Act 1929. The age for marriage was fixed at 18 for boys and 14 for girls. In 1949, the age was raised to 15 for girls and by an amendment in 1978, the age of marriage was fixed at 18 for girls and 21 for boys. Marriage in contravention of this requirement has been made an offence punishable with fine and/or imprisonment in varying degrees. The marriage, however, is not invalidated.[5]

It is significant to note that when the age for marriage for girls was raised to 15 by an amendment in 1949, there was a corresponding raise in the age for marital consent under section 375 of the Penal Code by an amendment in the same year. Thus sexual intercourse by a man with his wife, if below 15, constituted an offence of rape under the penal law. However, despite the amendment in 1978 raising the age for marriage to 18 for girls, the provision of marital rape in the penal code remains the same as in 1949, viz., 15.

The position under the penal law today stands thus. There is a wife not below the age of 15, there is one between 12 and 15 and there is still another, below the age of 12. So far as the first category is concerned, the exception to Section 375 of the Indian Penal Code says, "Sexual intercourse by a man with his own wife, the wife not being under 15 years of age is not rape." Thus if a wife is 15 or above, then whether or not she consents to the act, the husband cannot be held guilty of rape. If she is below that age, then the husband shall be guilty. However, here also, the law makes a distinction between a wife below 12 and a wife above 12.

Under section 376 where the wife is below 12, the penalty is severe; it is the same as provided for the offence of rape generally, viz., imprisonment of either description for a term which shall not be less than seven years but which may be for life or for a term which may extend to 10 years and shall also be liable to fine. If, however, the wife is not under 12 i.e. she is above 12 but below 15 (after 15 there is no offence at all) then the punishment is milder viz., imprisonment of either description for a term which may extend to two years or with fine or with both. Thus, we find that the law acquiesces in non-age marriages in several ways. Though pursuant to the Child Marriage Restraint Act, 1978, all the personal law statutes prescribe the age of marriage for a girl as 18 but except for the Special Marriage Act, 1954,[6] (which declares such a marriage as void) a marriage performed in violation of this requirement is valid in law.[7]

A Hindu wife, however, if she is married while below 15, may exercise her option of puberty by repudiating such marriage before she attains the age of 18.[8] If she chooses not to do so, the marriage is legal. Thus, marriage of a girl even before the age of 15 is tolerated, or rather 'compoundable,' one of the parties being the law itself. The only consequence is punishment under the Hindu Marriage Act,[9] or under the Child Marriage Restraint Act, 1978.[10] The penal code does not penalise the marriage of a girl above 15 even though she is below 18, for it explicitly exempts a husband from the offence of rape if his wife is 15 or above.

Marital Rape[2]

Of late our lawmakers have become sensitive to harassment of and atrocities on women. The insertion of cruelty—both mental and physical—as a ground for matrimonial relief, as well as in the Penal Code by way of a new section—498-A, and the enactment of various other special laws pertaining to women are a pointer to this. Marital rape, however, has been specifically exempted from the purview of criminal law.

According to a 17th century English jurist, Lord Mathew Hale, "The husband cannot be guilty of rape committed by himself upon his lawful wife, for by their mutual matrimonial consent and contract the wife hath given up herself in this kind unto her husband, which she cannot retract." Thus originated the matrimonial rape exemption principle in the common law which came to be cited frequently in marital rape cases.

The rationale behind this exemption was the doctrine of "unity in marriage." A man and a woman merged into a single legal being upon marriage and that being was the man. So, how could a man rape his ownself?

However, with revolutionary changes in the status of women, the rule of immunity for the rape of a spouse also came to be criticised. In America, since the 1970s there has been a change both in judicial attitudes and the rape laws. In 1984 a New York court[12] held marital rape exemption to be unconstitutional. Several countries, including the Soviet Union, Sweden, Denmark and Australia, allow prosecution of husbands for raping their wives.

However, under the Indian Law, as mentioned above, if a wife is 15 or above there is no rape even if she does not consent and the husband uses force. On the other hand if the girl is not the wife of the man but is below 16, then, even if she consents to the act of sexual intercourse, the man is guilty of the offence of rape.[13]

The Law Commission, in its *42nd Report* in 1971, had recommended that sexual intercourse by a man with his child wife, that is one below 15, should be taken out of Section 375 and made a separate offence. Consequently an amendment to the Penal Code was proposed in the Indian Penal Code (Amendment) Bill, 1972. The Joint Committee, however, took the view that intercourse by a man with his own wife, regardless of her age, should not be regarded as rape. Accordingly it deleted the proposed new section in Clause 157 of the Bill which sought to introduce the offence of marital rape. However, in case of a woman who is living separately from the husband under a decree of judicial separation or by mutual agreement, an amendment was approved. Section 376A was accordingly inserted. It says, "Whoever has sexual intercourse with his own wife, who is living separately from him under a decree of separation or under any custom or usage, without her consent, shall be punished with imprisonment of either description for a term which may extend to two years and shall also be liable to fine."

Among the arguments supporting marital rape exemption clauses—apart from the traditional concepts of implied consent on marriage or merger of entities are—that prosecution of a husband for raping his wife will be detrimental to marital harmony and also impede reconciliation efforts, that state intervention will be an invasion on marital privacy and that rape by a spouse is not as serious as rape by any other man.

It is also argued in favour of marital rape exemption that a complaining spouse has other available remedies under law like separation, divorce or claim for assault and that permitting women to prosecute their husbands for rape will open the floodgates for such prosecutions. Fear of fabricated and malicious complaints by wives who are not pulling on well with their husbands is another argument advanced by those favouring exemption.

These arguments are, however, not in consonance with latest social thinking and the principle of equality of the sexes in marriage. While sex is a natural concomitant of marriage, use of violence or force in sexual intercourse is an afront to the dignity of a woman's body and emotions whether it be in marriage or out of marriage. Though a husband's violent or non-consensual act of intercourse may entitle a wife to bring an action for criminal assault or injury or matrimonial relief, what is needed is the incorporation of the principle of liability for spousal rape in our penal law. In India, child marriages are still rampant despite laws against it. However, not only child brides but all wives need protection. The dignity and freedom of a woman over her body must be honoured. A marriage licence should not be viewed as a licence for a husband to forcibly rape his wife with impunity. Obviously, marriage does not mean a woman's consent to be raped by her husband ignoring her physical and emotional state.

NOTES AND REFERENCES

1. *Hindustant Times*, 16.12.1990.
2. (1891) 18 Cal. 49.
3. *Id.* at 62.
4. *Ibid.*
5. *Lila Gupta* v. *Lakshminarayan* AIR 1978 S.C. 1351.
6. Section 24 of the Act.
7. *Lila Gupta Supra* note 5.
8. Section 13(2)(iv) of the Hindu Marriage Act, 1955.
9. Under Section 18(a) of the Hindu Marriage Act, the punishment provided is simple imprisonment which may extend to fifteen days or fine which may extend to Rs. 1000 or both.
10. Under section 5 of the Act, the offence is punishable with simple imprisonment which may extend to three months and a fine.
11. *Indian Express*, 31.12.1991.
12. *People* v. *Liberta* 64 N.Y. 2d. 152 164, 474 NE 2d 567, 573 (1984).
13. Clause "sixthly" of section 375, Indian Penal Code.

FEMALE OFFENDERS

*Dr. S.K. Bhattacharyya**

Female offenders have only recently received some attention. In fact, their statistically meagre number and low security risk were a hindrance to the development of any progressive action towards custodial and processual justice to them. Moreover, the prison laws which are almost hundred years old, are not in keeping with the present trends in corrections, let alone the improvement of the conditions of female prisoners. At present, there are 1,280 prisons[1] in the country. Of these, only six are exclusively for women with a total capacity of 975. The annual average female prisoners population is about 4,000. Thus, only about one-fourth of the women prisoners can take advantage of these institutional facilities. It was in 1919 when the Indian Jails Committee for the first time brought into focus the importance of setting up separate institutions for women prisoners. Since then, the need for separate institutions for female prisoners has been emphasised at various forums. However, the Eighth Finance Commission has recommended Rs. 1,231 lakhs for the creation of separate jail capacity for 2343 women inmates.

Most of the undertrial female prisoners are lodged in separate enclosures of common jails. The All India Committee on Jail Reforms, 1980-83, expressed concern and observed : "It hardly needs to be argued that the principles underlying their confinement, should apply to their female counterparts also, with necessary adjustment for details issuing from sex differences. The fact, however, is that while living conditions, treatment and training for male prisoners are nowhere near the desired level, the lot of women prisoners is much worse. Women in prisons, as we have witnessed during our visits to various jails in different States and Union Territories suffer from unhealthy living conditions,

*Advocate, Supreme Court of India, New Delhi.

exploitation, unnecessary prolonged severance from their families and lack of gainful and purposeful employment."

It further opined that "in view of the status of women in the family and the society, their special needs and problems and their vulnerability while in prisons, special consideration has to be given to the segregation, protection, care, treatment, training and rehabilitation of women offenders." The committee made a number of important recommendations on various aspects of treatment and training of female prisoners. It also suggested that a woman's non-official organisation at the national level be set-up to look into the following issues :

1. Revision of legislation in respect of women prisoners;
2. Establishment of homes for released women prisoners;
3. Action against atrocities committed against women in prisons;
4. Re-integration of ex-women prisoners into the family and community;
5. Supply of free legal aid to women prisoners; and
6. Welfare of prisoners' family.

The problem relating to living conditions of prisoners arises due mainly to the overcrowding in hackneyed and dilapidated buildings. Most of the buildings in prisons in the country are more than half a century old. It is not feasible to conceive of the requisite standards of building, sanitary conditions, classification, education and training in crafts and other aspects of progressive treatment in the existing buildings. All types of prisoners including undertrials, convicts, casuals, habituals, juveniles, adult offenders, female offenders, mentally sick and physically handicapped are generally lodged in the same institution for their specialized treatment or training. The prevailing system of accommodating different categories of prisoners in the same prison has led to a lot of problems, especially in respect of women prisoners. While dealing with the problem of classification and segregation of female prisoners, the Indian Jails Committee, 1919-20, opined that "it is not only desirable to separate the convict from the unconvicted prisoner but it is also most necessary to keep female adolescents away from older prisoners, habituals from non-habituals, and prostitutes and procuresses from women who have lived hitherto a respectable life." Similarly, the All

India Committee on Jail Reforms, 1980-83, observed in its report that "segregation of offenders on the basis of sex, age, criminal record, social background, and sequence of criminal behaviour is an essential feature of modern prison system. But during our visits to various States and Union Territories we observed that undertrial prisoners, prisoners sentenced to short, medium and long terms of imprisonment, prisoners sentenced to simple imprisonment, habitual offenders, lifers, hardened and dangerous prisoners, children, young offenders, women offenders, civil prisoners, prisoners sentenced by court martial, criminal and non-criminal lunatics, detenus under the National Security Act, persons detained under the Conservation of Foreign Exchange and Prevention of Smuggling Activities Act, smugglers, etc., were all kept in the same institutions and the arrangements for their segregation even different wards were not effective." The National Expert Committee on Women Prisoners, 1986-87 has also brought into focus this problem and stated that in defiance of the correctional tenets, classification of prisoners continues to be non-existent in most prisons except in a few where longer-term sentence holders are kept. However, even in the latter, 'mental cases' along with those held under 'protective custody,' are indiscriminately mixed with other categories."

As a matter of fact, overcrowding in prisons is due to the presence of a large number of undertrial prisoners. According to the statistics for the year 1987, there were 4791 female prisoners out of whom 917 were convicts, 1836 undertrials and 595 civil prisoners and others.[2] Under such conditions, custody of inmates becomes the main concern of the staff, care and welfare of inmates is neglected. The total population of female prisoners far exceeds the existing accommodation available in separate prisons. If any meaningful programme is intended to be implemented, the buildings of the institutions should be properly designed and necessary accommodation provided.

The All India Jail Manual Committee, 1957-59 recommended that the prison population being diverse in terms of wide variations of intelligence and interest, it is necessary to organise diversified educational programmes to suit the needs of different inmate groups. Prisoners would be re-educated in order to assume total responsibility in the outside world. In pursuance of this recommendation, most of the States have introduced educational facilities in central and district jails. In some States, institutions provide facilities to selected inmates for attending schools or colleges outside. In spite of all these facilities, educational system in prisons needs further improvement in terms of diversification of the entire educational programme so as to cater to the varied educational needs of different groups of prisoners, particularly female prisoners. While discussing the problem of education for female prisoners in jails, the Indian Jails Committee, 1919-20 observed that "in the exceptional case of a female prisoner who is able to read, arrangements should be made to enable her to get books from the jail library should she desire to do so. It will hardly, we fear, be possible to arrange for regular instruction in the case of female convicts, except where special female prisons are provided."

The National Expert Committee on Women Prisoners 1986-87 while discussing the problem of work and education in prison observed that "both education and work are of proven value to prisoners and have an intrinsic role to play in the reclamation process not only during incarceration but also in the prisoner's rehabilitation after release." The Committee pointed out that "it is lack of education and work opportunity that is often responsible for the women's initial arrest as well as her deviance and custodialization." It went further to remark, "unfortunately, the inducements to advance educationally and to acquire an income generating potential have not found any systematic expression in the Indian custodial ethos." It may be possible to introduce condensed courses for those who desire to appear in secondary examinations. A majority of the female prisoners may not have the aptitude to go in for higher studies. So there should be an arrangement for training in crafts which are viable in the open community. Side by side, it is also essential to provide cultural and recreational activities in prisons for the benefit of the mental and physical health of female prisoners. These activities break the tedium of drab institutional regimentation and bring in an atmosphere of relaxation and joy. They are also intended to inculcate a discipline of healthy interests so that after release the inmate may spend her leisure time constructively. The effects of good recreational and cultural programmes may be as constructive as the products of education and vocational training. The All India Committee on Jail Reforms, 1980-83 recommended that 'suitable recreational programmes should be organised for women prisoners which may include simple outdoor games, bhajans, music, folk dances and drama. Those who have talent in any of these fields should be encouraged to develop and continue it.' These activities have sublime effects on the minds of prisoners and help in congenial personality development.

Vocational training is the important component of correctional treatment. The ultimate aim of all institutional training programmes is the rehabilitation of an inmate back into society. It enables a prisoner to acquire sufficient knowledge of any systematised craft so that she can earn a living on her own after release. It is often found that prison industries are so oriented that their main emphasis is not on training but production. As a result, the training aspect is neglected and this works as a handicap to the vocational resettlement of the inmate. As a matter of principle, there should be proper scientific classification of inmates in prisons. It is necessary to draw up suitable vocational training programme of each prisoner in accordance with her aptitude and interest.

The National Expert Committee on Women Prisoners 1986-87 suggested that "in existing prisons where women are in sufficient numbers a proper classification system must operate which should include medical, criminological and social assessment of the inmate and serve as a basis for specialised and segregated care, treatment, employment, training, education and rehabilitation of the inmate. In existing prisons with fewer inmates, scientific correctional care must be there even if physical segregation is not possible. The classification system should be introduced compulsorily in all prisons and custodial institutions. It should be used as a continuous programming and monitoring device rather than as a one-time activity." Training in some crafts as imparted at present in a number of institutions, has no relevance to the outside demands, and as such she has little chance of getting a job, leading to frustration. The All India Jail Manual Committee 1957-59, therefore, emphasised that 'Correctional Institutions should establish liaison with the Department of Technical Training and Vocational Guidance Institutes and After-care Agencies.' Such liaison would bring in improved efficiency in institutional training projects and practical utility from the point of view of the ultimate rehabilitation of inmates.

As regards medical facilities, women prisoners face problems because male doctors are generally posted in almost all prisons. So the National Expert Committee on Women observed, 'Medical, diagnostic and care facility must be available to inmates routinely and by a female doctor, where full or part-time women medical staff are ili-afforded, local female doctors from government health facilities must be inducted to serve the prisoners as visiting consultants.' The Committee went further to suggest that 'Schools of medicine should also be required to place women medical interns in prisons for specified periods'. Similarly, the All India Committee on Jail Reforms recommended that 'there should be a separate ward for women in prison hospitals. If there is no such hospital ward they should be treated in their own barracks by a lady doctor and attended to by female staff'. A female prisoner has special problems when she is found pregnant. Gynaecological examination needs to be conducted and pre-natal and post-natal care taken according to the requirements of each case. She has to be shifted to a local maternity hospital for purposes of delivery. If a birth takes place in the prison, the place of birth should not be mentioned in prison records as it may continue as a stigma for the child in the years to come. So it has been suggested by the All India Committee on Jail Reforms that 'instead the name of locality should be mentioned'.

A woman prisoner is allowed to keep her child with her in prison till it attains the age of 4 years[3]. Then the child has to be separated from the mother and sent to the members of the family at home or relatives, if any. Otherwise, there should be a separate family managed by trained staff specially appointed for this purpose. Although it will be entirely separated from the women's prison or annexe, all reasonable facilities may be extended to women prisoners to maintain contact with their children kept in the nursery. When these children attain the age of seven, they may be sent to the children's home which is to be set up by the Government for such purposes. The superintendent of the jail may move the juvenile court for committing the child to a juvenile home or a fit person, institution under the Juvenile Justice Act. During the Third Five Year Plan, a new scheme of welfare services in prisons was initiated as a plan scheme. This scheme included appointment of welfare officers in prisons and setting up of creches for children of female prisoners. The All India

Committee on Jail Reforms pointed out the inadequacies in this respect and suggested that children upto the age of five years accompanying women prisoners might be allowed to be kept with them and creches set up for these children outside the main prison building.

At present, prisons are manned mainly by custodial staff. In the majority of the institutions, professionally qualified correctional treatment personnel are not available, although in some States a beginning has been made by appointing social workers as prison welfare officers. These personnel can immensely help in realising their own drawbacks and remoulding their life-style through the methods of case work and group work. As a method of treatment, ties with the family and the outside community should be strong and in this respect the welfare officer has a very important role to play. Sometimes it so happens that during the incarceration, a prisoner loses contact with his relatives, friends and even her family members. Her emotional links get disrupted and she finds no interest in any aspect of programme in the prison. Under such circumstances, it is the task of the Welfare Officer to get her in touch with her friends and relatives. He may arrange for visits of her relatives and family members at regular intervals. He may discuss various problems that the prisoner apprehends, might stand in the way of her smooth rehabilitation and assist her in her overall planning, especially at the pre-release stage.

Although legal aid facilities are now available in some places, no significant steps have been taken to provide such facilities to women prisoners. In fact, a female prisoner suffers from a lack of knowledge of her basic rights and from the absence of a legal support system. What is worse, she is generally handicapped due to her illiteracy, low status and lack of independent capacity to mobilise resources. The family may shun her and may not like to defend her. Under such circumstances, there should be a legal aid unit attached to each prison to cater to the legal needs of women prisoners. The role of the Prison Welfare Officer is also important in keeping them abreast of the availability of such legal facilities. The National Expert Committee on Women Prisoners deliberated on this point and suggested that "to supplement the legal aid personnel, and to inject greater sensitivity to women's custodial situation, women social workers and activists need to be deployed and given appropriate para-legal training which should not only enable them to understand the legal aid processes but to utilise them to remedy existing lapses. Such a cadre of women workers can be reliably trained to deliver first aid in law to women in need both within and outside custody."

At the pre-release stage, the Prison Welfare Officer's assessment is essential for the prisoner's early release and also in arriving at a decision about her parole. However, this assessment is often delayed due to lack of adequate personnel and procedural reasons. As things stand at present, all the female prisons and female wards of prisons in various States and Union Territories do not have Prison Welfare Officers. In that case, Probation Officers of the district in which the prison is situated, may make an assessment of the prisoner well in time and suggest early release of the inmate or otherwise. The All India Committee on Jail Reforms 1980-83 recommended that 'special consideration should be given to women prisoners in the matter of their premature release.' To a matter of principle, the relatives of the woman who is about to be released from the jail, are to be intimated well in advance. If response from them is not encouraging, proper arrangement should be made for her return to the Community. It may be necessary for those who are homeless or rejected by their families to stay in a half-way-house for a particular period. In the pre-release and post-release programmes non-official organisations, especially women's organisations devoted to the field of welfare prisoners should be involved. In fact, a central committee for the assistance of released women prisoners should be set up in each State and local branches formed for each Central and District jail. These may be mainly non-official in character. However, the Superintendent of the jail and the District Judge as the Chief Judicial Magistrate of the district should be ex-officio members of the Committee.

After-care is a missing link in the process of treatment, training and rehabilitation of offenders. For after-care to be fully effective, it must be integrated with the work of the prisons in which the convict serves his sentence, and must be conceived as a process which starts on the convict's admission into custody, and is developed during his or her sentence. In fact, treatment in the prison and after-care should be part of the same process. According to Howard Jones, this process must begin as soon as the offender enters the prison and should not finish until the after-care officer ceases his activities with the ex-prisoner. The difficulties of an ex-prisoner are formidable and these are all the more acute in the case of a woman prisoner. The All India Committee on Jail Reforms 1980-83 deliberated on this problem observed, "Women offenders in India face peculiar problems of rehabilitation during their post-release period. Indian social customs make women ex-offenders more vulnerable to suspicion and rejection. The stigma of having been in a prison has much more adverse consequences for women than for men. The social system imposes many limitations on them and considers them outcasts. They are suppressed and forced to make compromises."

Although efforts were initiated in the early thirties to set up discharged prisoners aid societies in various states in the country, these could not be sustained due to the lack of patronage and community participation. Truly speaking, the institutional treatment programmes for prisoners cannot be successful unless well-organised after-care services are adequately available. In England, the Rehabilitation of Offenders Act, 1974 has been very effective in this respect. It provides that anyone who has been convicted of an offence and undergone a sentence of imprisonment of not more than two and a half years, is eligible for benefit under this Act. If he or she is not convicted again during the rehabilitation period, he or she becomes a rehabilitated person and his/her conviction becomes spent. The main advantage of this Act is that once a conviction has become spent under the Act, the convicted person does not have to reveal it. In fact, the previous conviction need not be disclosed while filling in an application form or at an interview of a job. Official records continue to be kept of spent convictions, but these may not be disclosed to others unless there is an official reason for doing so. In Britain, the after-care programme has been a good deal successful because prisoners are released from prisons on parole and licence and kept under supervision, till the term of imprisonment expires. During this period, the released prisoner has to abide by the rules and regulations prescribed under the law. If such a system with necessary legislation is introduced in India, the after-care programme may make much headway. Time and again, the problem of after-care of ex-convicts has been discussed at various forums and the necessity of introducing statutory after-care to facilitate rehabilitation of ex-convicts emphasised. In case of female convicts, statutory after care is all the more necessary to pave the way for their smooth rehabilitation in society.

In view of the present unsatisfactory plight of female prisoners, it is necessary to formulate a National Policy on Custodial Justice to Women as recommended by the National Expert Committee on Women Prisoners. In order to review the implication of the proposed policy, it suggested that a statutory autonomous body should be set up with representatives from each component of the criminal justice system and other disciplines like medicine, psychiatry, law, social work, etc. Since the beginning of this century, commendable efforts have been made to improve the conditions of prisons in the country by setting up Committees and Working Groups and a plethora of recommendations also remain on record. However, the main problem is the problem of implementation. Unless prison administration is included in the national development plans in its entirity, the cherished goal of transforming prisons as full-fledged therapeutic centres cannot be achieved.

NOTES AND REFERENCES

1. Report of National Expert Committee on Women Prisoners, Government of India, Ministry of Human Resource Development, Department of Women & Child Development.
2. National Institute of Social Defence, Government of India. Classification of female prisoners other than convicts was not reported by the States of Bihar, Gujarat, Nagaland and the Union Territory of Delhi.
3. The age-limit differs from State to State. In some States it is 5 years.

ABORTION : A SOCIO-LEGAL OUTLOOK

*Arvind Kaur** and *Shalini Marwaha***

Marriage is the union of two divinities that a third might be born on earth.[1] The mother-child relationship is the basic nexus and ultimate paradigm of human social relationships in India. It is the motherhood that the traditional family values and respects; wifehood and daughterhood are devalued and debased.[2] And it is rightly said that there are two kinds of unconditional love in this world—that of a mother for her child and that of a dog for its master. The woman has certain capacity and power which a man does not possess. It pertains to conception and delivery of children. She alone has the capacity to carry the child in her womb. Her service to society and the continuance of the human race is appreciable.[3] For the power to reproduce, a woman is worshipped, elevated to the position of a goddess. And yet it is the same function that can be used to reduce her to a slave, where she has no control even on her own body. In this regard, medical technology has been a mixed blessing for women. On the one hand, it has given them greater control over their bodies, through safe abortion, for instance; on the other, it has opened the possibility of repeated conception, and abortion[4].

Abortion is forcible expulsion of embryo from the womb before it can live on its own. The law no where uses the term 'abortion.' It only refers to miscarriage or termination of pregnancy. Before the passing of Medical Termination of Pregnancy Act (MTPA) in 1971 on the basis of the recommendations of Shantilal Shah Committee Report of 1966, which was set up by Family Planning Board in 1964 to make a study of illegal abortions, the Indian Penal Code allowed abortion of the foetus only

* Sr. Lecturer, Deptt. of Law, Punjabi University, Patiala.
** Lecturer, Deptt. of Law, Punjabi University, Patiala.

for the purpose of saving the life of the expectant mother.[5] The MTPA, which was passed to ensure better health and avoid risk to the life of the pregnant mother, has liberalised the law relating to abortion which has become popular as one of the means of birth control. The MTP rules which were framed in 1972 by the Government of India, exercising its power under section 6 of the MTP Act, were revised by the Central Government in 1975 on the recommendation of a workshop organised by the World Health Organisation (WHO) in New Delhi to implement the programme of medical termination of pregnancy even at district hospitals and at block level.

Section 3 of the MTPA facilitates a pregnant woman to terminate her pregnancy voluntarily[6] by a registered medical practitioner if the length of pregnancy is of twelve weeks. In case the length of pregnancy is between twelve and twenty weeks, then the concurring opinion of two medical registered practitioners is needed. An abortion is permitted if the doctor certifies that the continuing of the pregnancy would endanger the life of the pregnant woman or would affect her physical or mental health seriously or there is substantial risk of the child being born with physical or mental abnormalities or handicaps. The Act allows MTP facility not only to protect the mental health of the raped victim but also to a woman whose pregnancy is the outcome of the failure of a contraceptive device. Further, a woman can seek an abortion on the ground of her 'actual or reasonably foreseeable environment' being not conducive to her pregnancy.

It is a known fact that in spite of the existence of a liberal MTP Act which controls easy abortions, this facility is being misused through medical technology of amniocentesis. Amniocentesis is a technique which was initially developed to facilitate the detection of serious mental and physical abnormalities or other defects in an unborn baby during the advanced stage of pregnancy, i.e., around sixteen weeks of pregnancy. In this technique fluid is drawn by needle from the mother's amniotic sac and the cells in the fluid are cultured for diagnosis and tested. If any defect is detected then the foetus can be treated or aborted. So far as amniocentesis is used for detecting mental and physical defects in an unborn child it is perfectly justified but its use for the purpose of determining the sex of the unborn child through sex determination test is unjustified because it involves selective rejection of one sex, viz, a female child through abortion until the woman produces a child of the preferred sex, i.e., a male child. We cannot deny this harsh reality that ours is a society with obsessive and morbid pre-occupation with male progeny and blatant discrimination against females throughout their lives from the time of their birth. The practice of female infanticide was prevalent in India a long time ago though there are no references to this evil custom in the Vedic, epic or classical literature. This custom crept into some sections of Hindu society during the medieval period. But this never obtained a footing in cultural families. At the advent of the British rule, the custom seems to have prevailed to some slight extent in some lower sections of the society.[7] Now-a-days the practice of female infanticide is being resorted to in a more subtle and sophisticated manner, though it has been legally abolished a long time ago. It is an open insult to womanhood—the most sacrosanct and cherished institution. It is extremely detestable and abhorrent to the notions of a civilised society and grossly unethical. Indeed, it a structural and weird expression of violence towards women.

In the context of the provisions of Indian Penal Code and the MTP Act, abortion of female foetus does not hold any ground. It is also contrary to Article 51A(e) of the Indian Constitution which provides that it is the fundamental duty of every citizen "to renounce practices derogatory to women," and this practice is indeed against the female dignity. It amounts to culpable homicide. This practice is bound to have many adverse consequences such as imbalance in the male-female ratio of population and further deterioration of status of women which are already under-privileged.

Many women and health organisations have vehemently protested against this discriminatory practice. So far only the state of Maharashtra has responded to their protests by passing Maharashtra Regulation of the use of Pre-natal Diagnostic Techniques Act, 1988. This act does not ban amniocentesis as such, instead it provides for the regulation of use of this technique, solely for detecting genetic or metabolic disorders, chromosomal abnormalities or certain congenital anomalies or sex-linked disorders. The Central Government has not taken any concrete steps so far to form law on the lines of Maharashtra Act though it has stated that States can pass their own laws as health is a State subject.[8]

The complete ban on amniocentesis as such would be pointless because we cannot deny this fact that the abortion saves many unwanted children and agony of the birth of an abnormal or handicapped child but using this method for female foeticide is victimization of female bodies. It is a known fact that rarely does a woman undergo sex determination test voluntarily. In fact it is her circumstances which compel her to undergo it to resort to the demand that she produces a male child.

If the misuse of right of abortion has, on the one hand, led to female foeticide, then on the other, its exercise by woman without the consent of her husband has threatened her marriage and uprooted the very foundations of her matrimonial home. In an important judgement in *Sushil Kumar Verma* v. *Usha*[9], the Delhi High Court held that aborting the foetus in the very first pregnancy by a deliberate act without the consent of the husband amounts to cruelty within the meaning of section 13(1)(ia) of the Hindu Marriage Act, 1955. In this case, the wife aborted the foetus in a government approved pregnancy termination centre with the help of a registered medical practitioner after she became pregnant within one month of her marriage. Neither was the husband's consent taken nor was he enlightened about the pregnancy and the abortion. His petition for grant of a decree of divorce on the ground of cruelty was dismissed by the district court, but the Delhi High Court allowed it on appeal. Hence, the Delhi High Court's decision makes the husband's consent mandatory in matters relating to the termination of pregnancy. This judgement raises some crucial issues, such as :

(i) Whether a woman has right of control over her own body which includes a right to limit and space pregnancies.

(ii) Can an isolated act of an induced abortion by the wife without her husband's consent be stretched to such an extent as to include it under the concept of cruelty?

Indian Constitution does not explicitly mention right of privacy but it is implicit under Article 21 of the Constitution which grants right to life and personal liberty as one of the fundamental rights of its citizens. The Supreme Court's broad interpretation to this Article in many judgements enables to include right of privacy in it. Right of privacy includes to some extent activities relating to marriage, procreation, contraception, family relations, child rearing and their education. It is wide enough to encompass a woman's decision whether or not to terminate her pregnancy. Molly Yard, the President of the National Organisation for Women, said in reaction to decision in an American Case, *Roe* v. *Wade*[10] that :

> "If you can't control your reproductive system, you have no freedom."

In a society, men as well as women have strong parental feelings and it is even more strong in a woman's case. In fact, maternity is one of the most determinative aspects of a woman's life. It affects her physically as well as psychologically. But sometimes it disrupts her education, career and even her family life and an unwanted pregnancy may force upon her a distressful future life. The stress of giving birth to an unwanted child also reflects upon the bringing up of the child. So the woman has to be physically and mentally prepared for motherhood before taking a plunge on this line. Women should be allowed to have control of their bodies but the decision of Delhi High Court[11] states otherwise. According to it, a woman's right over her body is not unqualified and must be exercised with the consent of her husband. While delivering judgement in this case the Court has relied on the decision in an old English case, *White* v. *White*.[12] It has, however, failed to take notice of the fact that under present English law, consent of the husband is not necessary for abortion.[13]

In *Verma's* case, the court has also not bothered to take note of its own earlier decision in *Deepak Kumar Arora* v. *Sampuran Arora*,[14] wherein Delhi High Court has held that it cannot be laid down as a proposition of law that whenever wife undergoes an abortion without obtaining consent of the husband, it would *ipso facto* amount to cruelty. It may become necessary for physical or psychological reasons for a wife to undergo abortion.

The Delhi High Court in *Verma's* case further held that one of the primary ends of marriage is to have progeny and by aborting the foetus in the very first pregnancy the wife has vitiated the primary purpose of marriage.

We do not deny the importance of progeny in a marriage and it is also a fact that a child is part of both the parents.

Moreover, men are dependent on women to satisfy their paternal urge. But it is also a medical fact that abortion does not hinder future conceivement altogether. Pregnancy often comes more than once to the same woman. Hence, abortion is not synonymous to sterilisation or tubectomy.

In this case the court has also conveniently ignored the provisions of MTP Act 1971 along with the revised rules which allow a woman to abort without the consent of her spouse.[15] The husband of the patient need not be informed either.[16] The rules make it binding on the doctor performing the abortion to observe complete secrecy and protect the confidentiality of the patient by not entering the name of the patient any where else except the admission register and by destroying the admission register after the expiry of five years from the date of the last entry therein.[17] This decision also makes government's family planning propaganda futile of not having first child soon after the marriage, futile.

The issue of husband's consent from moral perspective and as father's right may be justified to some extent since it becomes useful in those situations, where a pregnant wife is not able to make a rational decision regarding keeping or terminating the pregnancy due to the fact of being not mentally prepared for motherhood. In such cases, the husband is the best person familiar with wife's condition. His presence adds new dimension to the case. But a rigid requirement of husband's consent do add to administrative responsibilities such as in cases of doubts regarding the identity of the husband. It can cause unreasonable delay which can be risky to the expectant mother as well as to the foetus.

Above all, making it a factor for dissolution of marriage causing cruelty, is highly anarchic and objectionable. And we should not forget the warning of Lord Denning that :

> "If the doors of cruelty were opened too wide, we should soon find ourselves granting divorce for incompatibility of temperament. The temptation must be resisted lest we slip into the state of affairs where the institution of marriage itself is imperilled."[18]

If, however, a wife undergoes abortion with a view to spite the husband or shows complete disregard to the husband's paternal feeling by refusing to have a child at all and keeps on aborting every time, then it may in such circumstances be contended that the act of getting herself aborted has resulted in cruelty to the husband. But such motives cannot be attributed to all cases where the husband is not consulted. It is an indisputable fact that a number of women put themselves to grave risk by undergoing abortions, though advanced medical echnology has made it easier.

Therefore, this is high time to stop indulging in 'slippery slope arguments' and to accept the crude facts of life that in certain cases as discussed above, right of abortion to a woman cannot be denied, but simultaneously with the help of the following measures not only can check be imposed on the misuse of this facility but also the law relating to abortion be made more offensive.

Suggestions

1. There is an urgent need for central legislation banning the misuse of amniocentesis technique for sex determination. Stringent punishment should be provided both to the guilty party and the abettor along with making it a cognizable and non-bailable offence.

2. Apart from the legal measures this pathetic situation can also be changed by restructuring the social outlook through public education. Since no law can be adequate in the cases where the question of social attitudes is involved which lay emphasis on inequality between the sexes, the objective can be effectively realised with the help of social welfare organisations supplementing the already existing governmental propaganda through media regarding the protection and care of girl child.

3. Under the Code of Medical Professional Ethics any doctor found guilty of misusing amniocentesis technique should as a penalty, be restrained from practising for a certain duration.

4. Lastly, in the light of Roscoe Pound's 'Social Engineering' notion, the law of abortion should be so interpreted by the courts as not to disturb the balance of the matrimonial life in the society. Therefore, it is submitted that there is need to review the decision of Delhi High Court in *Verma's* case and isolated exercise of right of abortion by a married woman even in the first

pregnancy unilaterally should not be strictly construed as basis of cruelty making it a ground for divorce.

NOTES AND REFERENCES

1. Khalil Gibran, *A Third Treasure*, ed. by Andrew Dib Sherfen.
2. Ashis Nandy, "Women Versus Womanliness : An Essay in Speculative Psychology", B.R. Nanda, ed. *Indian Woman from Purdah to Modernity*, p. 152-153.
3. Malladi Subbamma, *Human Rights—Women's Rights*—AIWC Publication 1.
4. Kalpana Sharma : "The Problem with girls", *Indian Express*, Dec., 1988.
5. Secs. 312 to 316 of the Indian Penal Code deal with abortion as crime.
6. If the woman is below 18 years or is a lunatic, the written consent of her guardian is necessary.
7. A.S. Altekar : *Position of Women in Hindu Society*, 7-8 (1987).
8. See Seventh Schedule, List II, Item 6 of the Constitution of India.
9. A.I.R. 1987 Del. 86.
10. 410 U.S. 113 : 35 L. Ed. 2d 147 dt 22-1-1978.
11. *Supra* note 9.
12. (1948) 2 All E.R. 151.
13. *Paton* v. *Trustees of B.P.A.S.* (1978) 2 All E.R. 987.
14. (1983) 1 DMC 182 (DB).
15. *Supra* note 6.
16. Rule 17 of Medical Termination of Pregnancy Rules 1971, as revised in 1975.
17. *Ibid.*
18. *Kaslefsky* v. *Kaslefsky* (1950) 2 All E.R. 398 at 403.

DAUGHTER'S RIGHT OF INHERITANCE UNDER ISLAMIC LAW —SOME REFLECTIONS*

*Kahkashan***

Under the Islamic laws of inheritance, a daughter gets a half share as compared to her brother who gets a full share in the parental property. Although at the time when these laws were given by the Prophet to this world, there was total justification taking into account the conditions prevailing. But today we are a part of an egalitarian society where the concept of equality has come as a breath of fresh air in the pleasant dawn of a new era after a dark and hopeless night. Society has freed itself from the shackles which were binding it to a parochial past and given a new thought to the changing dimensions of man-woman relationship.

Positive reforms in the direction of reforms in the Islamic laws of inheritance have been brought about in a number of Muslim countries and the same have been called for by a number of legal experts in India also. Basing his arguments on Section 2 of the Shariat Act, 1937,[1] Professor Z.M. Shahid Siddiqi has stated:

> "Agricultural land has been specifically exempted from intestate succession under Muslim Personal Law. The Quran and the Shariat do not distinguish between agricultural and non-agricultural land in terms of the property to be inherited. Inheritance includes the whole of the property of the deceased. Thus, by excluding agricultural land from intestate succession under the Quranic laws the legislature has made

* See in this context, Kahkashan, Rights of Inheritance of Women Under Islamic Law, *Woman Living Muslim Laws* (under print) for suggested reforms.

** Lecturer, Faculty of Law, Jamia Millia Islamia University, New Delhi a departure from the religious laws. The same method should therefore be applied in affording an equal share in the intestate's property to the females, that is a secular law should be enacted for this purpose as an exemption from the religious laws under the Shariat Act, 1937. Such an amendment will be in accordance with the spirit of religion in as much as we have seen that the purpose of the Quranic concessions to the females was to elevate their status from what obtained in the pre-Islamic days and to alleviate their burden."[2]

Quoting Professor Fyzee on changes in Islamic law of inheritance to give an equal share to the female heirs, Professor Sivaramayya has stated :

"Today in Islam this is the greatest difficulty. Shariat embraces both law and religion. Religion is based upon the will of the community as expressed by its legislature. Religion is unchangeable in its innermost kervel—But laws differ from country to country, from time to time. They must ever seek to conform to the changing pattern of society."[3]

He further says that there are two objections regarding reforms in Muslim Personal Law. These are (1) that the identity of the Muslim community will be effaced and (2) that public opinion among Muslims does not favour reforms which provide for equality of sexes.[4]

Replying to these objections he quotes Professor Fyzee as follows with regards to the first objection.

In the case of Muslims their identity has not to my knowledge been lost inspite of reforms in the Arab World, Turkey, Iran, Moracco and elsewhere.[5]

It is ironical that despite India having the second largest population of Muslims throughout the world, it is still lagging behind on the reforms. It is absurd to suggest that the identity of the community will be lost if they give an equal share to women in inheritance and that it will be preserved if an equal share is denied to them.[6]

As to the second objection relating to public opinion, reference is made to the research survey conducted by Professor Z.M. Shahid Siddiqi to find out whether women would like to have an equal share in the property by way of inheritance. It was revealed that out of the 50 Muslim women teachers who were interviewed as representative of the educated class, 65% of them complained that they have been denied their share in inheritance as ordained by the Holy Quran and the majority of the respondents demanded an equal share in the inheritance rights.[7] The right to equality in any case is an individual right and is not subject to control by members of a community.[8] Even otherwise when the Anglo-Indian legislations were enacted, there was no favourable public opinion, the laws were imposed upon the people and they still continue to be governed by them. So in matters of social reforms which are the need of the hour, instead of adopting escapist tendencies and hiding behind the curtain of religion one should have the courage to accept the challenge posed by the ever changing needs of the society and become more liberal in thought and action. Let us not deny the rights of a Muslim woman. Give her a due share according to the principles of equality and justice for she is your own daughter one of the very likes of Hazarat Fatima, the beloved daughter of Prophet Mohammad, who been conferred with the status of First Lady of Heaven (Khatoon-e-jannat) by the God Almighty. When a daughter can be elevated to the highest pedestal of dignity and honour, when she can be conferred with the highest status in the spiritual sense, why cannot we give the same daughter her due share of being an heir in the practical sense.

Apart from the Islamic laws of inheritance, further let us examine some tentative ways and means to do justice to one's heirs in the spirit of 'To each according to his or her needs.'

Let us take an example where in a family there is one son and a daughter. Let us look into the various ways and means by which the parents in the above example can attempt to do justice to their children. Apart from doing justice suppose the daughter in this case is not poor, but the parents want to give her a share equivalent to her brother or want to give her something more apart from her share under the Islamic laws of inheritance, how will they go about it.

1. Hiba or Gift

Under Islamic/Muslim law, a gift can be made of the whole of the donor's property and it may be made even to an heir. So a Muslim can make a gift of his property either movable or immovable during his life-time in favour of his daughter or son who is poor. Since under Muslim law, acceptance being an essential of a valid gift, problems can crop up. It might be sheer hard luck if the donee throws out the donor from the property so gifted in case of immovable property. So providing for such sad eventualities in the future, one can make a hiba of such portion of the property during his life time in favour of the heirs which would satisfy their needs.

2. Will

The power of a Muslim to dispose of his property by will is limited in two ways, first as regards the persons to whom the property may be bequeathed, and secondly, as regards the extent to which the property may be bequeathed. Where the bequest does not exceed the legal one-third and is made to a stranger—it is binding upon the heirs. A bequest in excess of the legal third may be validated by the consent of the heirs, similarly a bequest to an heir may be rendered valid by the consent of the other heirs.[9]

The policy of that law is to prevent a testator from interfering by will with the course of devolution of property according to law among his heirs, although he may give a specified portion as much as a third to a stranger.[10] The reason is that a bequest in favour of an heir would be an injury to the other heirs, as it would reduce their share, and would consequently induce a breach of the ties of kindred.[11] But it cannot be so if the other heirs consent to the bequest. The consent necessary to give effect to the bequest must be given after the death of the testator, for no heir is entitled to any interest in the property of the deceased in his life time.[12]

Hence a Muslim having immovable property can make a will giving more than one-third of the property to the needy heirs as compared to the other heirs who are well off, provided the other heirs give their consent at the time when the will comes into operation, that is, after the death of the testator. But in this case there is no guarantee that the heirs who have suffered a financial loss by virtue of 'the will' will give their consent at all. So practically speaking, if the other heirs refuse to give their consent to a bequest of more than one third to an heir, then the legacy will fail and the property shall devolve according to the laws of inheritance.

3. Family Wakf

Wakf-alal-aulad is a Muslim device to create a private trust in perpetuity. It has been regarded as a concealed means for the aggrandizement of a family which is in flagrant violation of the rule against perpetuity.[13] The Privy Council declared family wakf invalid, being against the public policy of not allowing a person to tie up the corpus of property in perpetuity and reserve its income for himself, for his children, descendants and kindred indefinitely.[14] The concept of family wakfs was strongly defended by the Muslim community. It has held that the Prophet proclaimed that one's family and descendants are fitting objects of charity and to bestow on them, and to provide for their future subsistence, is more pious and obtains great reward than to bestow on the indigent stranger. A wakf for alal-aulad is an enduring benefaction, an act of ibadat.[15] Hence the above decision was abrogated by the Mussalman Wakf Validating Act, 1913. Such family wakfs have been abolished or restricted in a number of Muslim countries like Egypt, Lebanon, Syria, Tunisia, etc. The decision of Privy Council is still the law in Kenya. But in India, such wakfs are still valid under the Wakf Validating Act, 1913 which has been given a retrospective effect by the wakf Validating Act, 1930—and are outside the purview of the Transfer of Property Act, 1882 by virtue of Section 2 of the Act.

A family wakf need not be created for all members of the family. It may be created for some members, male or female to the exclusion of others, generation after generation.[16]

Hence a Muslim can create a family wakf in favour of his daughter with respect to that portion of his property which shall satisfy her needs and requirements.

4. Other Methods

(a) In case of immovable property he can mortgage it to a bank and keep the money in joint accounts maintained with his poorer children. The joint account can be operated only by him during his life time. He can also put the money in a Fixed Deposit in the joint names of himself and his children in a bank with the interest payable to him. On his death, the heirs in the joint account or Fixed Deposit if he wants can redeem the mortgaged property after repaying the debt to the bank.

(b) If a person has only cash, then again he can open joint accounts or Fixed Deposits with his poorer children with the amount in the account payable to either or survivor. The surviving heir can get the money on his or her father's death.

(c) One can enter into a contract of sale with another party regarding his immovable property creating life interest for himself. He can deposit the sale proceeds in joint accounts to be maintained with his legal heirs whom he wants to help out. The account can be operated only by him during his life-time. On his death, the life interest will extinguish and the property will pass to the vendee and the money in the joint account to the concerned heir.

Hence, such are some of the ways and means suggested in this article whereby a Muslim can divide his property equitably without coming into conflict with the laws of inheritance. He can adopt any of the above mentioned methods to look after the interests of his daughters. Following the spirit of the Holy Quran a Muslim can do justice to his daughters who are indigent, deprived and who need help to sustain themselves in the manner —to each according to her needs.

NOTES AND REFERENCE

1. Section 2 of the Shariat Act, 1937 - Notwithstanding any custom or usage to the contrary (Save questions relating to agricultural land) regarding intestate succession—the rule of decision in case where the parties are Muslims shall be Muslim Personal Law.
2. Z.M. Shahid Siddiqi, "Muslim Women's Right to Inheritance," *The Indian Journal of Social Science*, Vol. 5, 331, (July, 1993).
3. Sivaramayya, *Women's Right of Inheritance*, MLJ Press, Madras, (1973), 178.
4. *Id.* at 183.
5. *Ibid.*
6. *Supra* note 2 at 332.
7. A research survey conducted by Prof. Z.M. Shahid Siddiqi, for the Indian Council of Social Science Research on actual availability of property rights to women in four religious communities namely Hindus, Muslims, Christians and Parsis.